Third Edition

bju press®

Greenville, South Carolina

Note:

The fact that materials produced by other publishers may be referred to in this volume does not constitute an endorsement of the content or theological position of materials produced by such publishers. Any references and ancillary materials are listed as an aid to the student or the teacher and in an attempt to maintain the accepted academic standards of the publishing industry.

SCIENCE 3
THIRD EDITION

Coordinating Author
Joyce Garland

Authors
Janet E. Snow
Nancy Wilkison

Contributing Authors
Sandra Bircher
Betty Doeppers

Project Editor
Naomi Viola

Designer
Linda Hastie

Project Manager
Roxana P. Pérez

Consultants
Brad Batdorf
Sandra Bircher
R. Terrence Egolf
Sharon Fisher
Bill Harmon
Elizabeth Lacy
Clare Payne
Sherri Vick

Bible Integration
Brian Collins
Bryan Smith

Cover Design
Elly Kalagayan

Cover Illustration
Aaron Dickey

Cover 3-D Illustration
Matt Bjerk

Photo Acquisition
Rita Mitchell
Susan Perry

Illustrators
Amber Cheadle
John Cunningham
Courtney Godbey
Preston Gravely
Dave Schuppert
Lynda Slattery
Heather Stanley
Del Thompson

Produced in cooperation with the Bob Jones University School of Education and Bob Jones Elementary School.

Photograph credits appear on pages 247–49.

© 2009 BJU Press
Greenville, South Carolina 29614
First Edition © 1976 BJU Press. Second Edition © 1989, 1996, 2003 BJU Press

ISBN 978-1-59166-846-6

15 14 13 12 11 10 9 8 7 6 5 4

OUR COMMITMENT.
YOUR CONFIDENCE.

CREATIVE
Updated look. Colorful,
interesting pages.

CREDIBLE
Thorough research. Solid content.

CHRISTIAN
Nothing to conflict with Truth.
Everything to support it.

WHEN YOU THINK TEXTBOOKS...
THINK BJU PRESS.

www.bjupress.com   1.800.845.5731

Contents

1

God's Many Creatures

Imagine if every time you grew enough to need new clothes, you also needed a new skin. Chapter 1 tells about animals that have to get new skins when they outgrow their old ones.

Some birds have wings but cannot fly. Instead they use their wings in other ways. Find out in Chapter 2 how a couple of these birds use their wings.

CHAPTER 1

In Psalm 145:10 the Bible says, "All thy works shall praise thee, O Lord." God's works are all that God has made. We can praise Him, but so can plants and animals. All things should bring Him glory.

Even small animals bring Him glory. Exodus 8 tells us that God sent frogs to cover the land of Egypt. The ruler of Egypt, Pharaoh, would not let God's people leave. God sent the frogs to punish Pharaoh. Pharaoh repented, and Moses told him that God would take the frogs away. By this Pharaoh would "know that there is none like unto the Lord our God."

Cold-Blooded Animals

God made our world and all that is in it (Genesis 1). He made the land and the water. He made plants of all kinds and sizes. He also made each kind of animal. Last of all, God made man. He named the first man Adam.

God gave Adam the job of naming the animals. What a big job that was! The Bible tells us in Genesis 2:19–20 that Adam named the cattle, the birds of the air, and the beasts of the field.

Scientists also give names to animals. Scientists put animals that are alike into groups. Putting animals that are alike into groups is called **classifying**. The scientists use how the animals are classified to give them names.

All animals fit into two big groups. There are animals that have backbones, and there are animals that do not have backbones. Animals with backbones are called **vertebrates**. Animals without backbones are called **invertebrates**.

Invertebrates

After a rainstorm, you may see earthworms wiggling on the ground. Worms are one kind of invertebrate. They do not have backbones.

There are millions of animals without backbones. They are many different sizes. Some can be huge. The giant octopus is an invertebrate. Other invertebrates are small. Crabs and clams are small invertebrates. Ants and spiders are even smaller invertebrates.

Some invertebrates live on land. Some live in the water. Wherever they live, they have one thing in common. None of them have backbones.

worm

crab

cricket

How are vertebrates and invertebrates different?

Vertebrates

Many animals do have backbones. These animals can also be big or small. Some fly. Others walk or swim. There are thousands of animals in the vertebrate group.

We can separate vertebrates into two smaller groups. Some vertebrates are warm-blooded. Others are cold-blooded.

Warm-Blooded Animals

Bears, cats, and seals are warm-blooded animals. Any animal that has fur or feathers is warm-blooded. A **warm-blooded** animal has about the same body temperature all the time. A cat may sit in the sun for a while. Later it might take a nap in the shade. The cat's body temperature stays about the same no matter where it is.

warm-blooded animal

Cold-Blooded Animals

Lizards, turtles, and frogs are cold-blooded animals. Cold-blooded animals do not have fur or feathers. They have scales or smooth skin.

A **cold-blooded** animal has a body temperature that changes depending on the surroundings. The animal's body is the same temperature as its surroundings.

When a lizard sits in the sun, it gets warmer. Its body temperature rises. When the lizard moves to the shade, it gets cooler. Its body temperature drops.

Cold-blooded animals get warm by being in the sunlight. The heat from the sun warms them up. They are more active when they are warm. When they get too warm, they have to cool off. They might find shade under a rock, or they might cover themselves in mud. Sometimes animals get into water to cool off.

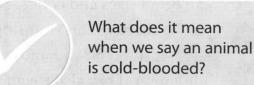

What does it mean when we say an animal is cold-blooded?

cold-blooded animal

7

Kinds of Cold-Blooded Animals

There are thousands of cold-blooded animals. All these animals can be classified into smaller groups. These groups are fish, amphibians, and reptiles.

Fish

Kinds of fish

Fish are cold-blooded animals that live in water. They hatch from eggs. There are many varieties of fish. Fish can be all sizes and colors. Some fish are small. Goldfish can be shorter than your fingers. Other fish can be very large. If stood on end, most swordfish are taller than an adult man. They also weigh more.

Clown fish are brightly colored. Other fish have darker colors. Cod and tuna are dark colored on top, but they are white or light colored underneath. This helps them hide from other fish that might eat them. A flounder can change colors to help it blend in better with the ocean floor.

Many fish live in the salty ocean. Some of them live in warm, shallow waters. Others, such as anglerfish, live deep in the ocean where it is very cold and dark.

Perhaps you live near a lake or river or have visited one. Some fish live in freshwater lakes and rivers. Maybe you have fished for perch or bass. These fish are freshwater fish.

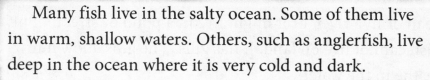

Science and the Bible

In Luke 5:1–11 the Bible tells about some fishermen. They had spent all night fishing, but they had not caught any fish. Jesus told them to throw out their nets again. When they obeyed, the nets filled with fish. There were so many fish that the boats began to sink! The fishermen were amazed at the miracle that Jesus had done. They knew He was God. When they got to land, they left their fishing nets and became disciples of Jesus.

What are three groups of cold-blooded animals?

Characteristics of fish

Many animals live in water, but not everything that lives in water is a fish. What makes a fish a fish? All fish have some of the same characteristics.

A fish lives its entire life in water. It may live in the ocean or in a river, or it might live in a pond or stream. But a fish cannot live on land. It has gills. The gills allow it to breathe in the water.

A fish also has fins that help it move around in the water. A fish's tail is a fin. The tail fin helps the fish move forward in the water. Its other fins mainly help the fish stop and rest without rolling over.

gills   **fins**

Creation Corner

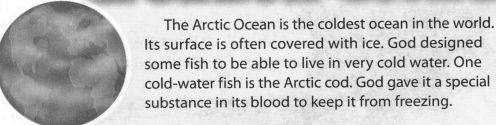

The Arctic Ocean is the coldest ocean in the world. Its surface is often covered with ice. God designed some fish to be able to live in very cold water. One cold-water fish is the Arctic cod. God gave it a special substance in its blood to keep it from freezing.

Fish have slimy, scaly skin. The slime is clear. It is not easily seen, but it can be felt. This slime helps fish move through the water easily. It also helps protect their skin from pests and infections. Touching a fish causes some of the slime to rub off. Without the slimy protection, the fish is more likely to get sick or injured.

Most fish have hard scales underneath their slime coat. The scales overlap each other and help protect the fish. God designed the scales to be strong, yet lightweight.

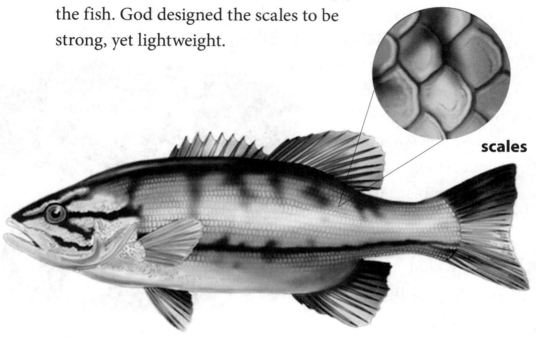

scales

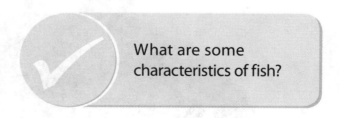

What are some characteristics of fish?

Amphibians

What is the difference between a frog and a toad? A frog has a narrow body and long back legs. A toad has a wider body and shorter legs. Though different in these ways, frogs and toads are alike in most other ways.

Characteristics of amphibians

Frogs and toads belong to the same group of cold-blooded animals. Salamanders also belong to this group. They are all amphibians. **Amphibians** are cold-blooded animals that live part of their lives in water and part of their lives on land. The name *amphibian* means "double life."

tree frog

salamander

Amphibians have smooth, moist skin. Because their skin is thin, they do not have to drink. They can absorb water through their skin.

Amphibians live in many places. Most amphibians live near water or in damp places. Others live on trees or under rocks and leaves.

toad

Life cycles of amphibians

When young amphibians live in water, they breathe through gills. Adult amphibians usually live on land. On land they breathe with lungs.

Young amphibians often do not look like adult amphibians. God designed amphibians to grow in a special way. Their bodies change as they grow. These changes are called **metamorphosis**.

Most amphibians lay eggs in water. A frog is an example of an amphibian that lays its eggs in water. The frog eggs hatch into tadpoles. The tadpoles grow and change. They lose their tails and grow legs. They also lose their gills and form lungs. Then the adult frogs can move onto land.

Stages of Metamorphosis

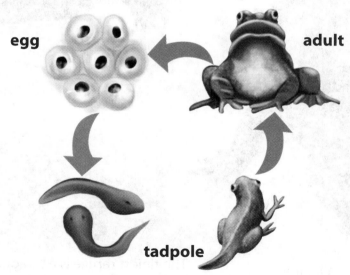

egg

adult

tadpole

What is an amphibian?

What do we call the changes that happen as an amphibian becomes an adult?

Reptiles

How are turtles, lizards, and snakes alike? All these animals are reptiles. Reptiles are another group of cold-blooded animals.

Characteristics of reptiles

Reptiles are cold-blooded animals with tough, dry, scaly skin. They breathe with lungs all their lives.

This group includes animals of many sizes. Some are very small. There are lizards that could fit on your finger. But this group also includes very large animals. Crocodiles and alligators are large reptiles.

snake

turtle

alligator

Fantastic Facts

The tiniest reptile is a Jaragua lizard. This lizard is so tiny that when it curls up it can fit on a dime. It can stretch out to its full length on a quarter. Scientists found several of these tiny lizards on an island in the Caribbean.

Reptiles live in different kinds of places, such as deserts and forests. They may also live in swamps or in the ocean. Reptiles that live in water still breathe with lungs. Some of them can stay underwater for more than an hour at a time. But they all must come to the surface to breathe air.

A reptile's tough, dry, scaly skin provides good protection. It helps protect the reptile from other animals that might want to eat it.

lizard

The skin also protects the reptile as it moves across the ground.

snake shedding skin

Many reptiles shed their skin several times a year. New scales grow underneath the old scales. This causes the old skin to loosen. Some reptiles, such as snakes, shed all their skin in one piece. Lizards and some other reptiles shed their skin in large strips.

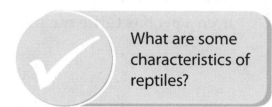

✓ What are some characteristics of reptiles?

Life cycles of reptiles

Fish and most amphibians lay their eggs in water. Reptiles lay their eggs on land. Some reptiles bury their eggs in the ground or make a nest in grasses. Other reptiles hide their eggs in rotten logs. Some sea turtles swim thousands of miles to lay their eggs on the same beach every year.

Most reptiles lay several eggs at one time. Some lay twenty or thirty eggs in their nests. Others lay more than a hundred eggs at a time.

Baby reptiles hatch from the eggs. The young reptiles look like adult reptiles but are smaller. They do not have gills as young amphibians do. They breathe with lungs as soon as they are born.

turtle's nest

Reptiles can live a long time. Some live as long as most people do. Giant tortoises can live more than 80 years, and even a pet box turtle can live for 40 or more years.

God's Power

Genesis 1 records God's power in Creation. God made the birds and the water animals on the fifth day of Creation. The next day He made the land animals. He did this just by the power of His words. He simply spoke, and all the animals were made.

God made a great variety of animals. No two are exactly the same. Even within the groups of fish, amphibians, and reptiles there are many differences. God planned and provided for each animal. He gave each animal the type of skin it needs and the lungs or gills it needs so it can breathe.

God alone has the power to create and take care of our world. In Matthew 10:29–31 the Bible says that even a sparrow does not fall to the ground without God knowing about it. We are of more value to God than the sparrows. Knowing this, we can trust Him to provide for us.

✓ Where do reptiles lay their eggs?

MEASURE UP
TEMPERATURE

A **thermometer** is a tool used to measure temperature. Cooks use thermometers to measure how hot foods are. A nurse might use one to tell whether you have a fever. Thermometers also measure how hot or cold it is outside.

One kind of thermometer has numbers along the side. The red liquid in the thermometer rises when it is measuring something warm. It lowers in the thermometer when something is cold.

The numbers on the side help us know the measurement of how hot or cold something is.

The set of numbers on the side of a thermometer is called a scale. Some thermometers measure temperature with the Fahrenheit scale. Other ones use the Celsius scale. Some thermometers have both scales written on them. Scientists usually use the Celsius scale to measure temperature.

To read a thermometer, look at the number next to where the red liquid stops. That number will tell you the measurement of how hot or cold something is. For example, this thermometer is in a cup of water. The red liquid stopped at the number 30. We would say the temperature is thirty degrees Celsius. You would write it as *30°C*.

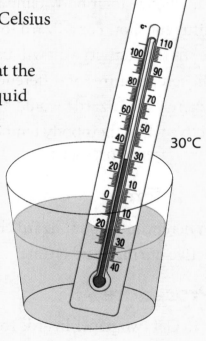

30°C

What is a thermometer?

Which temperature scale do scientists usually use?

ACTIVITY

Process skills
- Hypothesizing
- Measuring and using numbers
- Inferring
- Collecting and recording data

Leaping Lizards

Like all cold-blooded animals, lizards can change their body temperature by moving to a different spot. For a lizard to be active, it must be warm.

In this activity you will use thermometers to measure the temperatures of different areas. You need to find a spot where your "lizard" would be active. These "lizards" are active when their body temperatures are 21°C–31°C (70°F–88°F).

Problem

Where would your "lizard" be more active during the daytime?

Materials
2 paper lizards
crayons
scissors
tape
2 thermometers
Activity Manual

Procedure

1. Get two paper lizards from your teacher. Color and cut out the lizards.

2. Use tape to attach the thermometers to the lizards.

3. Complete the hypothesis in your Activity Manual.

4. Put the lizards outside in the morning. Place one in a sunny spot. This is your Sunny Lizard. Place the other in a shady spot. This is your Shady Lizard.

5. Wait 10 minutes. Then check each thermometer. Record the temperatures in your Activity Manual.

6. Leave the lizards in their places for at least two hours. Then check the thermometers again. Record the temperatures.

Conclusions

▶ Did the temperature change in the shady spot?

▶ Would your Shady Lizard have to move to a warmer area to be active?

Follow-up

▶ Check and record the temperatures every hour throughout a day.

Words to Know

classifying	cold-blooded	reptile
vertebrate	fish	thermometer
invertebrate	amphibian	
warm-blooded	metamorphosis	

Key Ideas

▶ Animals can be separated into two large groups: vertebrates and invertebrates.

▶ Vertebrates can be separated into warm-blooded and cold-blooded animals.

▶ Fish, amphibians, and reptiles are three groups of cold-blooded animals.

▶ Fish breathe with gills and have scales and slimy skin.

▶ Amphibians undergo metamorphosis as they grow. They have smooth, moist skin.

▶ The stages of metamorphosis for an amphibian are egg, tadpole, and adult.

▶ Turtles, lizards, and snakes are three kinds of reptiles.

▶ Reptiles lay their eggs on land and breathe with lungs.

▶ Scientists use the Celsius scale to measure temperature.

Write About It

Pretend you have found a new cold-blooded animal. Write a paragraph about it. Tell what group the animal belongs to. Describe what the animal looks like using what you have learned about that group of animals.

CHAPTER 2

The Bible speaks often of sheep and shepherds. When Jesus was born, angels appeared to shepherds who were watching their sheep. Other shepherds are also mentioned in the Bible. King David was once a shepherd of his father's sheep.

Psalm 23 compares God's care for His children to a shepherd's care for his sheep. Sheep are quite helpless. They are easily injured and scared. A good shepherd takes care of his sheep. He sees to their every need. The Bible tells us in John 10:11 that Jesus is the Good Shepherd, Who "giveth his life for the sheep."

Warm-Blooded Animals

Suppose you take your temperature while you stand outside in the hot sun. Then you go inside a cool building and take it again. Would your body's temperature be about the same in both places?

You may feel hot outside and cool inside. But your body temperature would not really change much. You are **warm-blooded**. This means your body temperature stays about the same no matter where you are.

God has given your body different ways to keep a constant temperature. When you are hot, you sweat to cool off. When you are cold, you shiver to warm up.

Many animals are also warm-blooded. Birds and mammals are warm-blooded animals. They have ways to keep their body temperature constant. Some mammals and birds shiver as we do. Dogs pant to keep cool. Birds fluff up their feathers to keep warm.

bird fluffing its feathers

dog panting

Birds

Birds are warm-blooded animals that have feathers. A bird's feathers help it stay warm. A bird's body makes a kind of oil that the bird spreads on its feathers. The oil helps make the feathers waterproof.

hawk

ostrich

penguin

Birds also have two legs and two wings. Most birds can fly. Wings and feathers help a bird fly, but a bird needs more than feathers and wings to fly. God gave birds a special bone structure. Many of their bones are hollow and lightweight. These hollow bones make the birds lighter.

Some birds, though, do not fly. The ostrich is the largest bird in the world. It cannot fly, but it can run fast. An ostrich uses its wings to help it change direction when running. The penguin cannot fly either. It uses its wings to swim.

What word means that a person or an animal has about the same body temperature all the time?

What are some characteristics of birds?

Nests and Eggs

Fish, amphibians, and reptiles lay eggs. Birds also lay eggs, but their eggs are different. Bird eggs have hard shells. Most birds lay their eggs in nests.

Bird eggs are different colors. Some are blue, brown, white, or gray. Others are speckled.

A nest of leaves and twigs might have speckled green or brown eggs in it. The eggs blend in with their surroundings. This blending in is called **camouflage**. It helps hide the eggs. Animals that want to eat the eggs might not see them.

Some birds' nests are camouflaged in trees or in tall grasses. Other birds hide their nests in the cracks of rocks.

brightly colored eggs

nest hidden in rocks

What do we call the blending in of something with its surroundings?

You can get to know about another person by talking with him. Most birds cannot talk to you. But you can get to know about birds by watching them.

In this exploration you will make a bird feeder. Observe the birds that visit your feeder. You will find out many interesting things!

What to Do

1. Make a bird feeder. Your teacher will give you the directions for how to do this.

2. Fill the feeder with food. Place the feeder near a window or in another place where you can easily observe the birds.

3. Observe the birds that come to the feeder. Record your observations on your own paper.

4. Keep the feeder clean and filled with food.

Characteristics of Birds

If you watch a bird feeder, you may see many kinds of birds. You may also see birds by a lake or at a park. You can observe the characteristics of birds to help you know what kinds of birds you are seeing.

Size and color

Birds are different sizes. The ostrich and emu are both very large birds. The adult ostrich is taller and heavier than most adult men. Hummingbirds are very small birds. Some are so small that one of them can fit in the palm of your hand. Most birds you see are larger than a hummingbird but much smaller than an ostrich.

hummingbird

God designed some birds to be camouflaged. Their colorings help them hide in the grass or in bushes. Other birds, such as bluebirds, have very bright feathers and wings. Birds may also have markings on their wings. A bird's coloring and markings can help you identify what kind of bird it is.

Sometimes the male and female birds look different. A male cardinal has bright red feathers, but the female cardinal is a plain reddish brown.

male cardinal
female cardinal

Songs and sounds

Sometimes it is fun to sit in a quiet place outside and listen to the birds. The chirping and tweeting of some birds are like songs. God has given each kind of bird its own sound.

The bobwhite quail gets its name from the sound that it makes. It sounds like it is saying "bob white." In the evening you might hear the hoot of an owl or the screech of a hawk. The mockingbird sings the songs of many other birds. It can even mock other sounds, such as the bark of a dog.

What are two things you can use to help identify birds?

Mammals

If asked to name an animal, you would most likely name some kind of mammal. Mammals are the animals that we know best. Most pets are mammals. So are most farm animals. There are several thousand kinds of mammals.

Mammals are warm-blooded animals that have hair or fur. Many mammals have hair or fur all over their bodies. Other mammals, such as elephants, have hair in just a few places.

Mammals live all over the earth. Bobcats and bighorn sheep often live in mountain areas. Camels and jackrabbits live in deserts. Foxes and bears live in wooded areas.

Most mammals have four legs, but not all mammals do. Some have fins or flippers instead of legs. Whales, dolphins, and seals are mammals without legs. They live in the water.

All mammals breathe with lungs. Mammals that live in the water can stay underwater longer than we can, but they still breathe with lungs. They must come to the surface to breathe.

bighorn sheep

jackrabbit

seal

Instead of laying eggs, almost all mammals give birth to live young. Many mammal babies are small and helpless at birth. Kittens and puppies are born with their eyes closed. They depend on their mothers for everything.

Some mammal babies, though, are not small or helpless. Baby giraffes can be as tall as an adult man! They can stand and run soon after they are born.

Mammal mothers feed their young with milk. All mammal babies depend on their mother's milk for a while. Some mammals, such as mice, are ready to be on their own in just a few weeks. Other mammals stay with their mothers for months or even years.

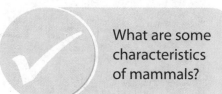

What are some characteristics of mammals?

There are many kinds of mammals. They all have hair or fur and breathe with lungs. Even so, they can be very different from each other.

Hoofed Mammals

Many mammals have hooves. The hoof is the hard part of the mammal's foot that touches the ground. It helps protect the animal's feet. Farm animals such as cows, goats, horses, and pigs have hooves. Deer, buffalo, camels, and giraffes also have hooves.

Marine Mammals

Some mammals spend most of their time in the water. Mammals that live in the sea are called **marine mammals**. Dolphins, whales, and seals are marine mammals. This group also includes sea otters and manatees.

sea otter

dolphin

zebra

Flying Mammals

Bats are the only mammals that can fly. There are bats that fly around during the daytime, but most bats sleep during the day and are active at night. Bats live in dark places. They usually make their homes in caves, rocks, and trees. They often hang upside down when they are resting.

yak

pig

manatee

bat

Is a zebra a hoofed mammal or a marine mammal?

What mammal can fly?

Climbing Mammals

Climbing mammals spend much of their lives in trees. This group of mammals includes monkeys, gorillas, and lemurs. These animals usually have hands that can grasp and hold on to things. Many of them have long tails. Monkeys often use their tails like an extra arm or hand.

lemur

Gnawing Mammals

Some mammals have large front teeth. Their teeth never stop growing! They have to gnaw, or chew, on things to keep their teeth worn down and sharp. Squirrels, mice, and hamsters are gnawing mammals. Porcupines and beavers are also part of this group.

beaver

Hunting Mammals

Hunting mammals chase and eat other animals. The big cats, such as lions and tigers, are hunting mammals, but so are pet cats. You may have seen a pet cat chasing a mouse or bird. Dogs are also hunters. Wolves and coyotes are types of dogs.

wolf

Pouched Mammals

Some mammals have pouches outside their bodies. Their babies grow and develop inside these pouches. Mammals with pouches are called **marsupials**. Kangaroos, opossums, and koalas all have pouches.

kangaroos

Humans

Humans have the same characteristics as mammals, but humans are not animals. In Genesis the Bible tells us that God made man in His own image. Because we are made in the image of God, we can have fellowship with Him.

We can worship God with our prayers.

Animals' bodies die. Our bodies die also, but we will live somewhere forever. God sent His Son, Jesus, to die for us so we can live forever with Him. Humans are special to God.

What are pouched mammals called?

Why is man not an animal?

Behaviors

Perhaps you have seen a dog shake hands or do other tricks. You may have seen a service dog do tasks for its owner. Those are all examples of learned behaviors. Someone taught the dogs to do those things. A **learned behavior** is something that an animal learns to do.

Many animals learn new behaviors. Birds learn to come to a feeder for seeds and nuts. Dolphins learn to search for things in the water. A chimpanzee might learn to crack nuts by seeing another chimpanzee smash a nut with a rock.

There are other behaviors, though, that animals do not have to learn. Birds are born knowing how to build a nest. Dolphins and whales are born knowing how to swim. These are instincts. **Instincts** are the basic knowledge and skills that an animal is born with. Animals need instincts to survive.

This dog was trained to help its owner.

This dolphin was taught to do tricks.

This bird was born with the instinct to build a nest.

Man can teach animals many things. Animals also teach each other and learn by experience. Instincts, though, cannot be taught.

God gave each animal the instincts it needs. He gave some animals, such as cats, the instincts to hunt and eat meat. To other animals, such as birds and bats, He gave the instinct to fly. He provided exactly what each animal needs to live.

✓ How are learned behaviors different from instincts?

Science and the Bible

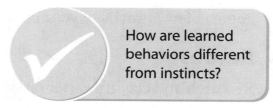

In Daniel 6 the Bible tells of a time when God kept some lions from following their instincts. A law was made that people could pray only to the king. Daniel was a servant of God. He refused to stop praying to God. He was thrown down into a lions' den, but God closed the mouths of the lions. They did not eat Daniel. The king took Daniel out of the lions' den. The lions were hungry, though. The men who had told the king about Daniel's praying were thrown into the den. The lions attacked the men before they even fell to the bottom.

ACTIVITY

Animal Books

You probably are familiar with many mammals. But there are other animals that you might not know much about. In this activity you will research, or look up facts about, a few animals of your choice.

Purpose

Research and classify vertebrates.

Procedure

Materials
Animal pages
resources about animals
glue or tape
folders with brads

1. Choose three vertebrates that you would like to know more about.

2. Write the name of each animal on one of the *Animal* pages.

3. Look up information about each animal. Find out where the animal lives and what it eats. Record that information on that animal's page.

4. Decide which vertebrate group each animal belongs to. Record the group for each animal.

5. Find a picture of each animal. Cut out the picture and glue or tape it on the animal's page.

6. Find two interesting facts about each animal. Record those facts.

7. Share your *Animal* pages with your classmates.

8. Organize all the pages by the groups the animals belong to. Put each group of *Animal* pages into a different folder. Write the name of the animal group on the front of each folder.

9. Display your animal books.

Conclusions

▶ How did you know which animals fit into each group?

Follow-up

▶ Add more animals to each book.

Words to Know

warm-blooded   mammal   learned behavior

bird   marine mammal   instinct

camouflage   marsupial

Key Ideas

▶ Birds, mammals, and humans are warm-blooded.

▶ Birds have feathers and hollow bones and lay eggs. Most can fly.

▶ Bird characteristics such as size, color, and sound help us identify birds.

▶ Mammals have fur or hair, breathe with lungs, give birth to live young, and feed their young with milk.

▶ God made many kinds of mammals, including hoofed, marine, flying, climbing, gnawing, hunting, and pouched.

▶ Humans have characteristics of mammals but are not animals. God made man in His own image.

▶ Instincts are given by God.

Write About It

A zoo has an area called Marine Mammals. Write a paragraph telling what animals you might find there. Also name one way their area would be different from the areas of other mammals.

2 God's Great Design

Most trees are green during the growing season of the year. Many seem to put on other colors in fall. But not all things are as they seem. Find out in Chapter 3 what makes the fall colors appear.

Many animals eat other animals for food. Did you know that some plants can also eat animals? Chapter 4 tells about a couple of these plants.

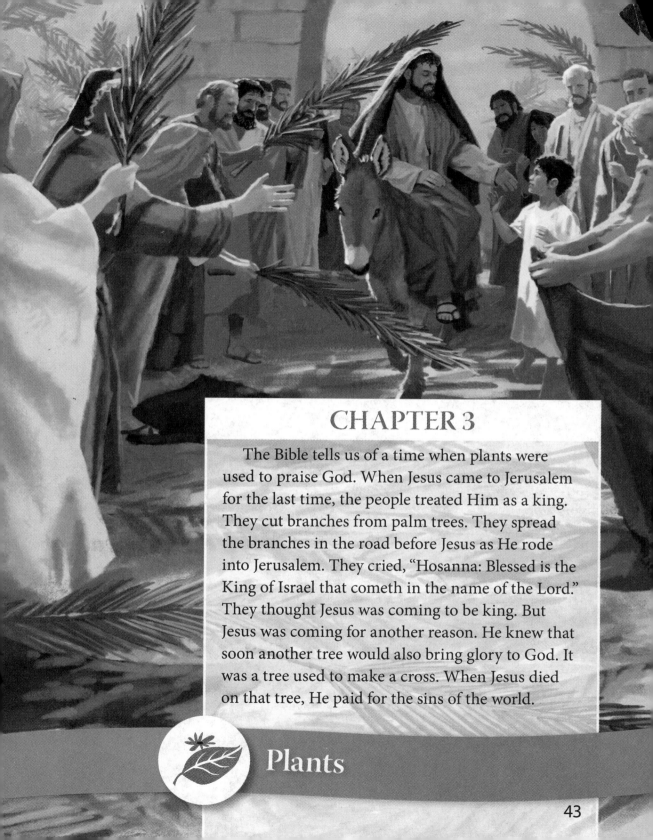

CHAPTER 3

The Bible tells us of a time when plants were used to praise God. When Jesus came to Jerusalem for the last time, the people treated Him as a king. They cut branches from palm trees. They spread the branches in the road before Jesus as He rode into Jerusalem. They cried, "Hosanna: Blessed is the King of Israel that cometh in the name of the Lord." They thought Jesus was coming to be king. But Jesus was coming for another reason. He knew that soon another tree would also bring glory to God. It was a tree used to make a cross. When Jesus died on that tree, He paid for the sins of the world.

Plants

If you take a walk in a forest, you might see many animals. Birds fly from tree to tree. Squirrels chase each other up and down tree trunks. Spiders spin webs from branch to branch. Rabbits nibble on low bushes.

Animals are living things. They use energy to move around and do things. But animals are not the only living things using energy in the forest. They are not the only ones doing something. The trees and other plants are also doing something. They are making food.

Plants

A plant is a living thing that makes its own food. A rabbit can hop from one place to another to get food, but a plant cannot get up and move to find food. It must be able to get what it needs without moving from place to place.

Plants have different parts that help them get what they need to make food and grow.

Parts of a Plant

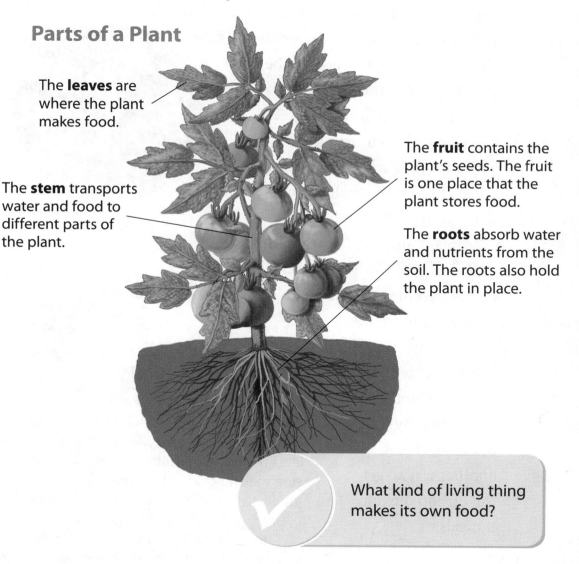

The **leaves** are where the plant makes food.

The **stem** transports water and food to different parts of the plant.

The **fruit** contains the plant's seeds. The fruit is one place that the plant stores food.

The **roots** absorb water and nutrients from the soil. The roots also hold the plant in place.

What kind of living thing makes its own food?

Making Food

God gave plants a special way to get the food they need. **Photosynthesis** is the process plants use to make food. A plant needs sunlight, carbon dioxide, and water for photosynthesis to happen.

Sunlight is a form of energy. It is the energy that the plant uses for photosynthesis. Most photosynthesis happens in the leaves of a plant. Leaves have very tiny parts called **chloroplasts**. These chloroplasts are the parts of the plant that help the plant make food.

In the chloroplasts is a green coloring called **chlorophyll**. Chlorophyll is what makes plants green. The chlorophyll absorbs, or takes in, the sunlight.

chloroplasts

A plant also needs carbon dioxide to make food. Carbon dioxide is a gas that is part of the air. To take in gases that we need from the air, we breathe with our lungs. A plant does not have lungs, but God gave it another way to get the carbon dioxide it needs.

Fantastic Facts

In the fall we may say that the leaves are changing color, but they really are just showing less green. Some plants, such as maple trees, stop making chlorophyll when temperatures begin to get cold. Without chlorophyll the leaves begin to lose their green color. Other colors start to show. The leaves are then red, orange, or yellow.

Plant leaves have tiny openings called **stomata**. These stomata are on the underside of the leaves. The stomata open and close to allow carbon dioxide into the plant.

stomata

The third thing a plant needs to make food is water. The roots of a plant absorb water. Then small tubes carry the water from the roots to the stems and leaves of the plant. These small tubes are called *xylem*.

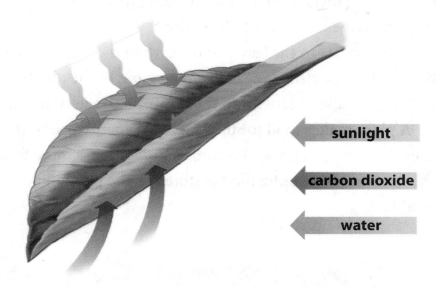

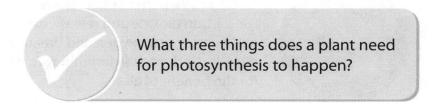

sunlight

carbon dioxide

water

✔ What three things does a plant need for photosynthesis to happen?

Using Food

During photosynthesis, a plant takes in sunlight, carbon dioxide, and water. The plant then uses these things to produce food and oxygen.

The food that the plant makes is a type of sugar. Tiny tubes called *phloem* carry the sugar to all the parts of the plant. The sugar becomes food for the plant. It provides energy, which the plant uses to grow.

The oxygen that the plant makes is a gas. Like carbon dioxide, oxygen is a part of the air. It is the gas animals and humans need to breathe to survive. Plants release the oxygen they make into the air. By doing this, they help provide oxygen for other living things.

The stomata in the leaves allow carbon dioxide to enter the plant. They also allow oxygen to go out of the plant. Extra water also escapes into the air through the stomata.

A plant makes food to supply its own energy needs. It uses the energy to grow. But sometimes it makes more food than it needs. The extra food is stored in the plant to be used later.

Creation Corner

God has a perfect plan for His creation. Plants use carbon dioxide and release oxygen. Animals and humans use oxygen and breathe out carbon dioxide. God made living things to work together for the benefit of all.

Photosynthesis

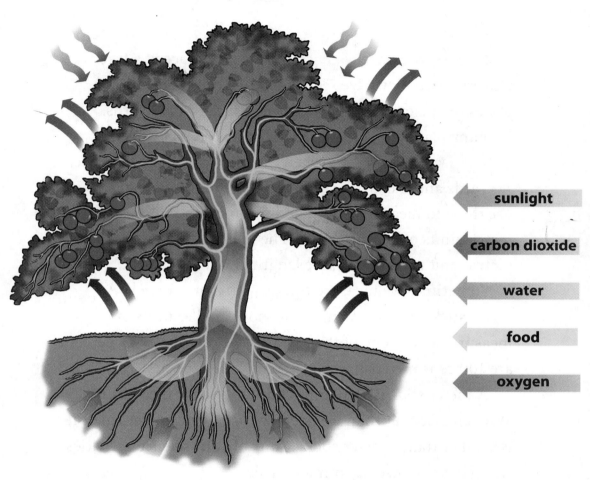

sunlight

carbon dioxide

water

food

oxygen

What two things does a plant produce during photosynthesis?

MEASURE UP
LENGTH

Perhaps you have watched people run a race at a track. One race you may have seen is a very short race. In some places the distance of the race is measured as 110 yards. In many places the race is measured as 100 meters. The 110-yard race and the 100-meter race are the same distance.

Yards and meters are both units of measurement. We use them to measure length and distance. In science we use metric units of measurement. The **meter** is the standard metric unit used to measure length and distance.

Sometimes we measure things with a meter stick. A meter stick has marks on it that show smaller units of measurement. Some of these marks are *centimeters*. There are 100 centimeters in 1 meter.

A meter stick is sometimes hard to use for measuring. When it is longer than we need, we use a centimeter ruler. It is smaller than a meter stick. Many of your science activities will tell you to use a centimeter ruler.

A centimeter ruler has centimeters and millimeters marked on it. *Millimeters* are even smaller than centimeters. There are 1,000 millimeters in 1 meter. The centimeters and millimeters on a centimeter ruler are used to measure short lengths. Some rulers have centimeters marked on one side and inches marked on the other side.

When you measure, place the ruler next to the object you are measuring. Line up the zero mark on the centimeter ruler with one end of the object. Look at the centimeter number closest to the other end of the object. If the object's length is between two centimeter marks, choose the closer mark.

For example, the length of the pencil shown below is 15 centimeters. The length of the pen is between 14 and 15 centimeters. It is closer to 15, so we would say that the pen is 15 centimeters long.

The pencil is 15 centimeters long.

The pen is 15 centimeters long.

What standard metric unit do scientists use to measure length and distance?

ACTIVITY

A Time to Grow

Plants need light to make food. But will they grow without light? In this activity you will compare the growth of two plants to find out whether darkness affects plant growth.

Problem

Does a plant need light to grow?

Procedure

Materials
2 plastic cups, 9 oz
potting soil
2 seeds
water
centimeter ruler
Activity Manual

1. Label one cup *Light* and the other cup *Dark*. Put potting soil in each cup.

2. Plant one seed in each cup. Carefully water each seed the same amount. Observe the plants for several days. In your Activity Manual, record the date you see each plant poke out of the soil. Water the plants as needed.

3. Place the Light cup where it will get sunlight. Place the Dark cup in a dark place.

4. Measure each plant every day. Carefully place the end of the ruler on top of the soil. Measure the full height of the plant. Be careful that you do not pull the plant out as you measure it.

5. Observe the color and leaves of each plant.

6. Record your measurements and observations in your Activity Manual.

Conclusions

▶ Which plant grew taller?

▶ In what other ways are the plants different? What caused the difference?

Follow-up

▶ Repeat the activity with a different type of plant to see whether you get the same results.

Uses of Plants
Food

One way animals and humans use plants is for food. All living things need energy. Plants make food for their own energy needs, but they also provide energy for other living things. Plants store extra food. Animals and humans can eat the parts of some plants to get the stored energy.

God made many wonderful plants for us to eat, but we don't always eat the same part of the plant. Sometimes we eat the roots of plants. Carrots, turnips, and sweet potatoes are all roots we eat.

Celery is a stem that we eat. We can eat the stem of the broccoli plant, but we also eat its flowers. The ends of broccoli stems have florets, or unopened flowers, that we eat.

We eat the leaves of some plants. Lettuce, cabbage, and spinach are all plant leaves.

roots

stems

leaves

stems and flowers

54

Seeds are another part of the plant that we often eat. Nuts, beans, and peas are seeds. Wheat, oats, and corn are also seeds that we eat.

The part of the plant that we most often eat is the fruit. You can probably think of many kinds of fruit, such as apples, oranges, and pineapples. But squashes, cucumbers, and tomatoes are also fruits. A fruit is the part of a plant that contains the seeds.

God has made many wonderful plants for us to eat. He designed plants not only to make their own food but also to store food for other living things to use.

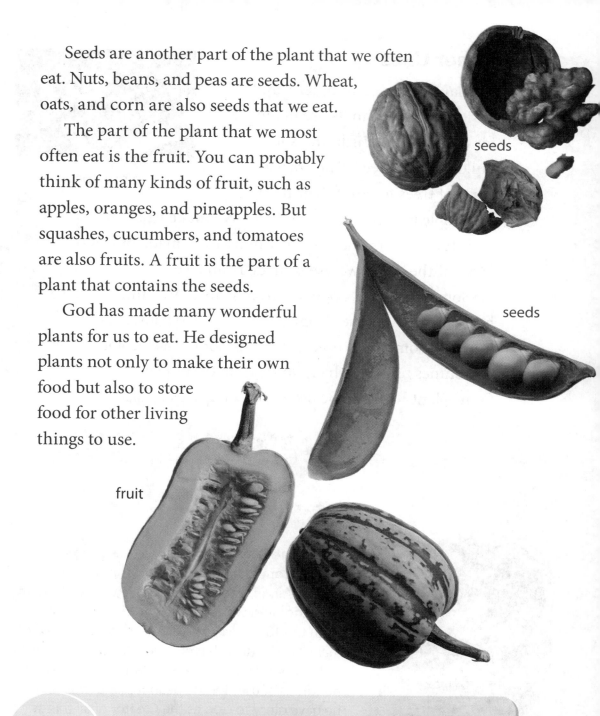

seeds

seeds

fruit

How do animals and humans get energy from plants?

Which part of a plant contains the seeds?

Other Uses

Plants are used in other ways besides food. Animals use plants for their homes. Birds and squirrels build nests in trees. Beavers use parts of trees to build their homes.

animal home

People use trees in many ways. We make wooden furniture. The frames of many houses are made of wood. Most of the paper we use is made from trees.

Some medicines are made from plants. A common heart medicine comes from a plant called foxglove. Aloe is a plant sometimes used to treat minor burns. People sometimes use witch hazel to treat small skin cuts. Some plants can also be used to calm upset stomachs.

aloe plant

paper

Meet the Scientist
George Washington Carver

George Washington Carver was born in the 1860s. From an early age, he was interested in plants. Carver wanted to learn. He worked hard to get schooling wherever he could.

In the 1890s insects were destroying the South's main crop, cotton. Carver suggested planting peanuts instead of cotton. He became famous for finding hundreds of uses for the peanut plant. In all his work, he gave glory to God as the Creator of all things.

Many of our clothes are made of fibers that come from plants. Cotton fibers are used to make cotton fabric. Cotton is a common fabric used for clothing. Most sheets and towels are also made of cotton.

Scientists continue to find new ways to use plants. They use plants to make plastics that will break down after they are used. This causes less pollution than regular plastics do. Scientists have even found ways to use some plant crops to make fuel that can be used by cars.

God gave us plants to use and to enjoy. We can relax in the shade of a tree. We can smell the fragrance of a flower. We can see the beautiful colors of the plants around us. Plants are a wonderful gift from God.

Ethanol is a fuel made from plants.

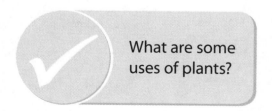

What are some uses of plants?

Words to Know

leaf	root	chlorophyll
fruit	photosynthesis	stomata
stem	chloroplast	meter

Key Ideas

▶ Plants use sunlight, carbon dioxide, and water to make their own food.

▶ During photosynthesis, plants produce food and oxygen.

▶ All living things need energy.

▶ Plants produce a kind of sugar as food. They use some food for their own energy needs, and they store the rest.

▶ Animals and humans eat plants to get the stored energy.

▶ Many foods that humans eat come from different parts of plants.

▶ Animals use plants for houses.

▶ Plants are used by people for many different things.

Write About It

Suppose you are planting some small flowers in your yard. Write a paragraph explaining why it would be important not to damage or destroy the leaves of the flowers as you plant them.

CHAPTER 4

When one part of God's creation changes, other parts change. The Bible tells us about a time when the Israelites turned away from God. They started worshiping idols. Because of their idolatry, Elijah, a prophet of God, prayed that it would not rain.

For three years it did not rain. The grass did not grow. The horses and mules began to die. The king and his governor went looking for water. God sent Elijah to meet the men. Elijah told the king that God would show Himself to be the only God. When the people saw God's power, they gave praise to God. Elijah prayed, and it rained.

Ecosystems

How can you tell if something is alive? Maybe it breathes. Perhaps you see it move. There are different ways to tell whether something is alive. All living things have some of the same characteristics.

Living things grow and develop. Living things also reproduce, or make more living things. For example, a tiny puppy grows quickly. Soon the puppy becomes an adult dog. Later this dog might have puppies of its own. Plants also reproduce. Plants make seeds, and new plants grow from seeds.

Living things interact with things around them. A dog might find shelter when it rains. It acts a certain way because of what is happening to it. The same dog might bark and chase other animals. The other animals may hide or run away. They act that way because of the dog.

Even plants interact with things around them. A plant grows toward sunlight. Plants take in and give off gases that are part of the air.

Ecosystems

Living things use some resources that are not alive. A resource is anything that meets the needs of a living thing. Both animals and plants need air and water. Many living things need sunlight. We call the things that are not alive the environment. The **environment** includes all the nonliving things that surround a living thing. Water, air, sunlight, soil, and temperature are parts of the environment.

A rainforest is an ecosystem.

Living things and their environment make up an ecosystem. An **ecosystem** is all the living and nonliving things in a certain area. Ecosystems can be big or small. A tropical rainforest and the animals that live in it make up an ecosystem. An ecosystem could also be a pond or a desert. Even your backyard is an ecosystem!

What is one characteristic of a living thing?

What is an ecosystem?

Living Together

Ecosystems usually have many kinds of animals and plants. A swamp ecosystem could include grasses and cypress trees. The swamp could also be a home for catfish, wood ducks, and alligators. Deer and foxes might live in parts of the swamp. These plants and animals are part of this ecosystem.

All the catfish in the swamp make up the catfish population. A **population** is all the plants or animals of the same kind that live in an ecosystem. A wood duck is not part of the catfish population. It is part of the wood duck population.

Populations can be different sizes. Hundreds of catfish may live in the waters of a swamp. The catfish population of that swamp ecosystem is quite large. The same swamp may have only a handful of deer. The deer population is much smaller.

Each population has a place to live, or a **habitat**, in the ecosystem. The alligators spend most of their time in the water. The alligators' habitat is the water of the swamp. Since the water is also a habitat for cypress trees, the alligators and trees share a habitat. Many populations can share a habitat.

Deer live in the woods of the swamp. Their habitat is the woods. Foxes also live in the woods. They share their habitat with the deer population.

All the different populations make up a community. A **community** includes all the living things in the ecosystem. For a swamp, the community includes the cypress trees and other plants. It also includes the catfish, wood ducks, foxes, and deer. All the living things are part of the community.

What is a population?

What is a community?

Eating for Energy

Living things need energy to live. Plants get energy from sunlight. They use that energy to make their own food during photosynthesis.

Plants are living things that can make their own food. Some of the food they use for their own needs. They store the rest of the food. Animals and people eat plants and get energy from that stored food.

Living things can be put into three main groups: producers, consumers, and decomposers. Plants are **producers**. They produce, or make, food that other living things need.

producers

Animals and people are **consumers**. They must eat plants or animals to get energy. They cannot make food for themselves.

consumers

Decomposers help break down dead things and wastes. Breaking down dead things and wastes adds useful substances called nutrients to the soil. Plants then use the nutrients to grow and produce more food.

Most decomposers are very small. Many of them, such as bacteria, are so small you cannot see them without a microscope. A few kinds of decomposers are larger. Mold and mushrooms are both decomposers. Earthworms are also decomposers.

decomposers

What do producers do?

What do decomposers do?

Types of consumers

Animals eat different things. Some animals, such as mice and elephants, eat only plants. Animals that eat only plants are called **herbivores**.

herbivore

Herbivores eat different parts of plants. Some herbivores, such as gophers, eat the roots of plants. Giraffes and koalas eat leaves. Zebras and sheep eat the stems of grasses. Sparrows eat the seeds and fruit of plants. Butterflies drink nectar from flowers. God designed each herbivore to get the energy it needs from the parts of plants that it eats.

Some consumers eat both plants and animals. These consumers are called **omnivores**. Bears, skunks, and robins are omnivores. Bears eat other animals, such as fish, insects, and small mammals. But they also eat grass, berries, roots, and nuts.

Fantastic Facts

Not all carnivores are animals. Plants such as butterworts and Venus flytraps "eat" insects and spiders. These plants still get energy from the sun, but they grow in places where the soil has few nutrients. The insects and spiders provide some of the nutrients the plants need.

omnivore

Many omnivores change their eating habits when the seasons change. For example, a skunk eats whatever is available in its habitat. In the winter skunks often eat rats and small mammals. During spring and summer, skunks eat plants and insects. In the fall skunks add fruits and berries to their diet.

Other consumers eat only other animals. They are called **carnivores**, or meat eaters. These animals get their energy by eating other consumers. Wolves, weasels, tigers, and some large birds are carnivores.

carnivore

What is a herbivore?

How is an omnivore different from a carnivore?

Food chains

A blade of grass produces its own food through photosynthesis. A grasshopper gets food as it nibbles on the blade of grass. Later a garter snake catches and eats the grasshopper.

The sun provided energy for the grass. That energy then passed from the grass to the grasshopper to the snake. This moving of energy through an ecosystem is called a **food chain**.

A food chain begins with the sun. The first living thing in a food chain is always a producer. A producer uses sunlight to provide energy for itself. The next link in a food chain is usually a herbivore. The animals that make up the other links of a food chain are predators. A **predator** is any animal that hunts and eats other animals. Predators can be carnivores or omnivores. The animals that a predator hunts are called its **prey**.

Food Chain

A food chain has only a few links. Each living thing uses some of the energy and stores the rest. The grass got energy from the sun. The plant used most of that energy to grow. Only some of the energy was stored.

The grasshopper ate the grass and got the stored energy. The grasshopper used most of that energy for its own needs. Some of the energy was stored in the grasshopper's body. The garter snake then came along and ate the grasshopper. When it did, the garter snake got the grasshopper's stored energy.

Each living thing uses most of the energy it gets for its own needs. That is why a grasshopper has to eat more than just one blade of grass. It needs the energy from many plants. Likewise, a garter snake needs to eat more food than just one grasshopper.

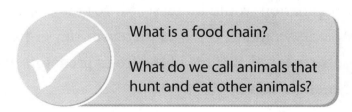

What is a food chain?

What do we call animals that hunt and eat other animals?

Food webs

A food chain shows only one source of food for each animal. Most animals, though, eat more than one kind of food. To show this, we use a food web. A **food web** is made up of several food chains linked together.

For example, a grasshopper eats plants, and a garter snake might eat the grasshopper. That is one food chain. In the same community another food chain might also start out with plants and a grasshopper. But in that food chain a frog might eat the grasshopper. The frog might then be eaten by a fox. The grasshopper is prey for both frogs and snakes. It is part of more than one food chain.

The fox is a predator for frogs. It is also predator for snakes and grasshoppers. It will even eat plants. The fox might be part of many food chains. A food web shows many prey and predator links.

When one part of a food web changes, it affects the whole food web. Frogs eat grasshoppers. If there were fewer frogs, fewer grasshoppers would be eaten. The grasshopper population would increase. More grasshoppers means more plants would be eaten. If there were fewer frogs, it would also mean that some of the frog's predators would not have enough to eat.

Food Web

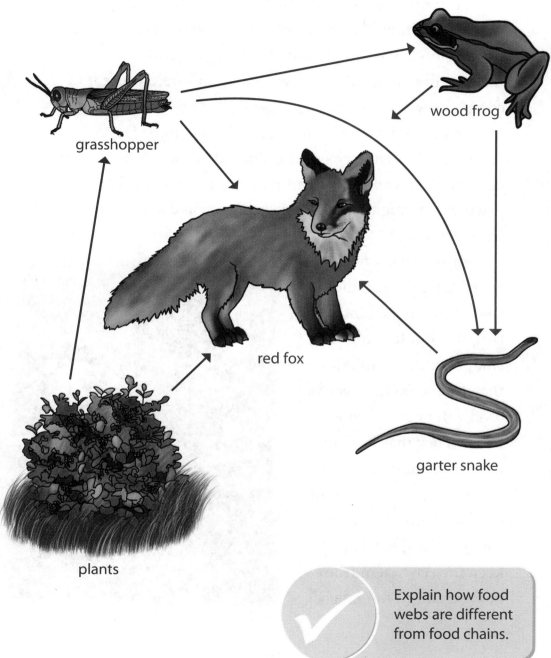

grasshopper

wood frog

red fox

garter snake

plants

Explain how food webs are different from food chains.

Changes in an Ecosystem

Ecosystems are always changing. Population sizes may change in an ecosystem. A disease may destroy a certain plant population. Animals that eat that plant may not have enough food. They might move to another ecosystem. The increase in animals in the new ecosystem would cause it to change as well.

Sometimes it is the environment that changes. Heavy rains can flood an ecosystem. The extra water might destroy plants and cause animals to move to another place. Not enough rain can cause dry soil and keep plants from growing.

People can change an ecosystem. If fishermen catch a lot of one kind of fish, its population gets smaller. Other animals that depend on that fish for food will not have enough to eat. They may have to move to another area. In some places there is a limit on how many fish can be caught. The limit helps keep the ecosystem from being changed too much.

Sometimes animals cause ecosystems to change. Beavers build dams across streams. The dam stops the flow of the water and turns the stream into a pond. After a while, the pond dries out and becomes a meadow.

God created living things with the ability to adjust. He also gave each plant and animal certain characteristics to help it survive in its environment. Animals might move to find more food or water. Deer grow thicker coats of fur when the temperature gets colder. Plants that live in dry areas usually have long roots. The long roots help the plant get water from deep in the ground.

Long-tailed weasels are usually brown, but some weasels that live in northern areas grow white fur during the winter.

 What kinds of changes can happen in an ecosystem?

Balance in an Ecosystem

Changes happen to the environment and to living things. Even a small change can cause many other changes. But God is a wise Creator. He planned for ecosystems to change and to balance each other.

Lightning can start a fire that burns a forest. Many habitats are destroyed in the fire. Plants and animals might be killed. Changes like these may seem sad or scary, but God uses them to renew ecosystems. Soon new plants start to grow. Animals that left may return to the area. Other animals also come live in the new ecosystem. Over time a new forest grows. It is somewhat like the forest it replaced, but it is also different.

A fire causes changes in an ecosystem.

God uses predators to keep an ecosystem in balance. Predators help control population sizes. An ecosystem can support only a certain number of living things. The number of living things that an ecosystem can support depends on the resources available. Animals that cannot find all the resources they need either move to a new place or die.

predator and prey

We live in a world of sadness and death. When humans first disobeyed God in the Garden of Eden, God cursed the world (Genesis 3:17–19). The sadness and death we see are a result of sin against God.

Revelation 21:4–5 tells us that when God reveals His new heaven and new earth, there will not be any more death. God promises us that He will make all things new and perfect. If we trust Jesus to take away our sin, God will make us part of that new and perfect world.

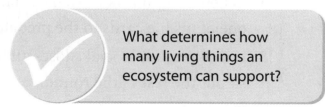

What determines how many living things an ecosystem can support?

Ecosystem Tag

Animals in a community interact with each other. Some are the prey. Others are the predators. But all are important to the balance of an ecosystem.

In this activity you will represent a kind of animal in an ecosystem. The different animals in this game of tag represent animals that interact in an ecosystem.

Purpose

Model animal interactions in an ecosystem.

Materials
identity badge
life cards
2 large plastic hoops

Procedure

1. Get your identity badge. Pick up the correct number of life cards for your animal.

2. Chipmunks and snakes need to avoid being "eaten," or tagged. Snakes can eat chipmunks. Owls can eat snakes and chipmunks.

3. Chipmunks are safe from their predators only when they are in a "den." Only one chipmunk can be in a den at a time, and he can be there for only 10 seconds.

4. When a chipmunk or snake is tagged, he must give up one of his life cards to the predator who tagged him.

5. If a chipmunk or snake loses all his life cards, he must sit out the rest of the round.

6. Play until your teacher tells you to stop. As a class, form three groups—one for each kind of animal.

7. Count your group's life cards. Tell that number to your teacher and turn in your identity and life cards.

8. Play the game again.

Conclusions

▶ Did each kind of animal have the same number of life cards left each time you played? Why or why not?

▶ What would happen if the entire population of snakes died?

Follow-up

▶ Add a "disease" player who can tag any animal, including owls.

Words to Know

environment	producer	carnivore
ecosystem	consumer	food chain
population	decomposer	predator
habitat	herbivore	prey
community	omnivore	food web

Key Ideas

▶ Living things grow, reproduce, and interact with the things around them.

▶ Food chains and food webs show how energy moves through an ecosystem.

▶ When one part of a food web changes, the change affects the whole food web.

▶ Ecosystems are always changing.

▶ God made living things able to survive in their environments and to change as things around them change.

▶ The number of living things in an ecosystem depends on the resources available.

Write About It

Pine beetles can kill the pine trees in an ecosystem. Write a paragraph explaining how that might affect other parts of the ecosystem.

3 God's Mighty Forces

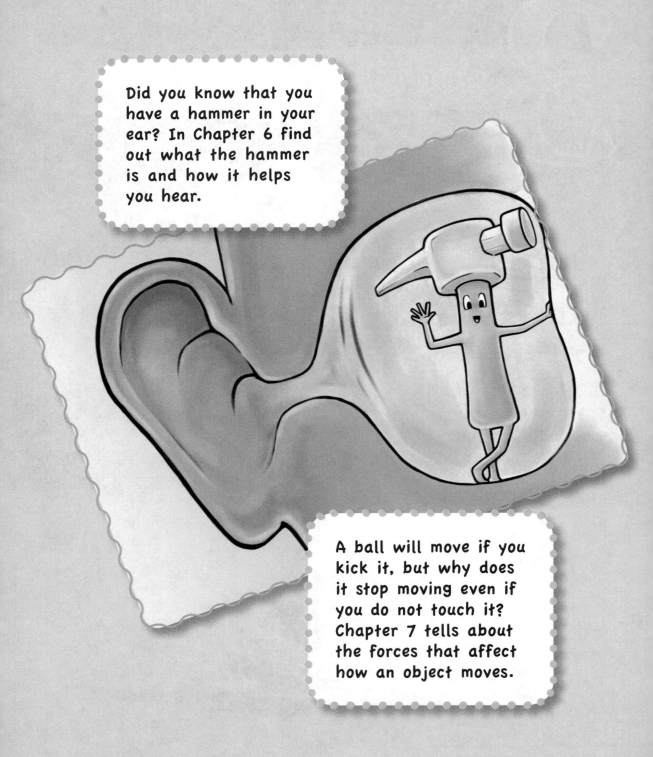

Did you know that you have a hammer in your ear? In Chapter 6 find out what the hammer is and how it helps you hear.

A ball will move if you kick it, but why does it stop moving even if you do not touch it? Chapter 7 tells about the forces that affect how an object moves.

CHAPTER 5

Sometimes we use things from God's creation in a way that is sinful. The children of Israel at one time gave their gold jewelry to be used in a wrong way. They melted their jewelry down to make an idol. The children of Israel gave glory to the idol of gold. God was displeased and punished them.

Later the people gave their gold for another offering. They gave to provide for the tabernacle. The tabernacle was a place to worship God. Many of the objects in the tabernacle were covered with gold. God was pleased that His people gave Him glory by building a beautiful place of worship.

Matter

What is in your bedroom? You probably have a bed and clothes in your room. Maybe you also keep toys, books, games, and sports equipment in your room. Perhaps you even have a pet fish or hamster. Your room has many things in it. All those things are types of matter.

Matter is anything that has mass and takes up space. Beds, balls, and fish are matter. The water in a fish bowl is also matter. The air in a balloon is matter. Even the air that fills a room is matter. It takes up space.

Matter has certain characteristics, or properties. You can observe those characteristics and use them to describe matter. Baseballs are round and hard. A stuffed bunny has a different shape and is soft and floppy. Shape and hardness are two properties of matter.

Properties of Matter

A **physical property** is a characteristic of matter that can be observed with our senses. Color, size, and shape are physical properties. Mass and volume are also physical properties.

All matter has mass. **Mass** is the amount of material that an object has. Some objects have more mass than others do. Often a larger object will have more mass than a smaller one, but mass does not depend on size. A baseball is much smaller than a beach ball, but the baseball has more mass.

Volume is another property of matter. **Volume** is the amount of space something takes up. Some things, such as a moving truck, take up a lot of space. The volume of a moving truck is quite large! Other things, such as a toy truck, take up only a little space. All matter has both mass and volume.

The moving truck has more volume than the toy truck.

What is matter?

What is a physical property?

MEASURE UP
MASS

Matter can be measured. One way we measure matter is by measuring its mass. Mass is a physical property that does not change. It stays the same unless matter is added or removed.

For example, you can change the shape of a lump of clay. You can roll it into a ball or smash it flat. You can shape it into a long rope. The clay's shape can change, but you still have the same amount of clay. Its mass did not change.

We use a balance to measure mass. A **balance** is a tool used to compare an unknown mass with a known mass. The object you are measuring has an unknown amount of mass. Balances have either sliding weights or a set of weights to use as the known amount of mass.

triple-beam balance

A triple-beam balance is a balance that has sliding weights. The object is placed on a plate on one side. The weights are slid along a beam. When the beam is balanced, the weights show the mass of the object.

A double-pan balance has a set of weights and two pans. The object you are measuring is placed in one pan. The known weights are added to or removed from the other pan until the line on the scale is level, or straight. When the two pans are balanced, the mass of the object equals the mass of the known weights.

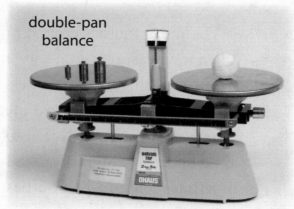

double-pan balance

The **gram** is the basic unit of measurement for mass. The clay in the pictures has a mass of 45 grams. The clay has a small amount of mass, but some things have much more mass. The mass of larger objects is measured in *kilograms*. One kilogram is equal to 1,000 grams.

This animal's mass is measured in kilograms.

What tool is used to measure mass?

What units of measurement are used to measure mass?

MEASURE UP
VOLUME

Volume is another property of matter we can measure. When we measure volume, we are measuring how much space something takes up.

The **liter** is the standard metric measurement for volume. Soft drinks are often sold in 2-liter bottles. The liquid takes up 2 liters of space inside the bottle. Water is sometimes sold in 1-liter bottles.

Smaller amounts of liquid are measured in *milliliters*. It takes 1,000 milliliters to equal 1 liter. You could not pour 1 liter of water into a mug. A mug holds about 240 milliliters.

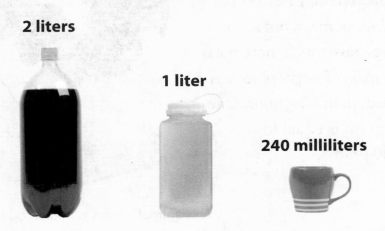

2 liters

1 liter

240 milliliters

Volume is measured with a graduated container. A **graduated container** has lines and numbers on its side. The numbers allow you to measure how much space a liquid takes up. A kitchen measuring cup is a kind of graduated container.

Suppose you need to measure 400 milliliters of water. You would first set the graduated container on a flat surface. Then you would pour water into the container until the water level is at the line for 400 milliliters.

We use volume to measure liquids, but you can also find the volume of a solid. For example, you can use water to find the volume of a small rock. First measure a volume of water. Then put the rock in the water. The rock should be totally under the water. The water level goes up because the rock takes up space. To find the volume of the rock, subtract the volume of the water from the final volume.

Suppose the water level went from 300 milliliters to 400 milliliters. Adding the rock made the water level increase 100 milliliters. The rock took up 100 milliliters of space, so the volume of the rock is 100 milliliters.

What tool is used to measure volume?

What units of measurement are used to measure volume?

States of Matter

Matter can be a solid, a liquid, or a gas. These are called the states of matter. Each state of matter has certain properties. Matter is grouped into states by these properties.

Solids

Blocks, books, and baseballs are solids. A **solid** has a definite shape and volume. You can put an apple inside a box, but the apple is still round. It does not change its shape to fit the shape of the box. It keeps its own shape.

The volume of a solid also stays the same. Even when you cut the apple into pieces, all the pieces together have the same volume as the whole apple did. Its volume does not change.

Some solids, such as glass and tables, are hard, but solids do not have to feel hard. A blanket and the fur of a cat or dog are also solids.

A solid has a definite shape and volume.

Liquids

Water, milk, and oil are all liquids. A **liquid** has a definite volume but not a definite shape. A liquid takes the shape of whatever container it is in.

Milk in a tall, thin glass takes the shape of the glass. But pouring the milk into a short, wide bowl makes the milk change shape. The volume of the milk does not change, but the shape of the milk does. A liquid can have different shapes, but its volume does not change.

A liquid has a definite volume but not a definite shape.

Which state of matter has a definite shape and volume?

Which state of matter has a definite volume but not a definite shape?

Gases

The air in your bike tires is a gas. The helium in a balloon is also a gas. A **gas** has no definite volume or shape.

Like liquids, gases take the shapes of their containers. The air in a tire takes the shape of the tire. If you pump air into a soccer ball, the air takes that shape. If you pump the same amount of air into a football, the air takes that shape.

Gases are different from solids and liquids. Gases expand, or stretch out. They fill the space of a closed container. A gas keeps expanding until something stops it. That something may be any kind of container or closed space. A tied balloon and a sealed jar are examples of closed spaces.

A gas does not have a definite shape or volume.

You can use a balloon to compare how liquids and gases fill a container. When you pour water into a balloon, all the water goes to the bottom. As long as you do not tip the balloon, the water does not come out. When you blow air into a balloon, the air does not all go to the bottom. Instead, the balloon inflates evenly. If you do not pinch the balloon shut, the air will expand and escape out the hole.

Solid	Liquid	Gas
Keeps its shape	Takes the shape of its container	Takes the shape of its container
Keeps its volume	Keeps its volume	Takes the volume of its container

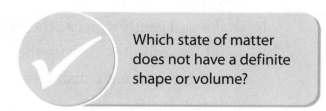

Which state of matter does not have a definite shape or volume?

Frozen Treats

What is your favorite dessert? Is it a solid or a liquid? Some desserts, such as gelatin, go from a liquid to a solid. In this activity you will observe what happens when a liquid mixture becomes a solid.

Purpose

Observe a liquid change to a solid.

Procedure

1. Measure 240 mL of milk and pour it into the small bag. Measure the sugar and vanilla. Add them to the milk.

2. Close the bag. Gently squeeze and shake the bag until the milk, sugar, and vanilla are mixed together. Set aside.

3. Fill the large bag about half full of ice cubes. Measure and add the salt.

4. Put the small bag inside the large bag and close the large bag.

5. Shake and gently squeeze the bag with your fingers for about five minutes. Be sure the bag stays closed. If your hands get cold, put a dish towel between the bag and your hands.

Materials

metric measuring cups
metric measuring spoons
resealable plastic bag, pint size
240 mL milk
30 mL sugar
2.5 mL (1/2 tsp) vanilla flavoring
resealable plastic bag, gallon size
ice cubes
120 mL salt
dish towel (optional)
2 bowls
2 spoons

6. Observe what happens inside the small bag as you shake the large bag. Discuss your observations.

7. After five minutes, take the small bag out. Open it and divide the contents into two bowls. Observe how the contents are different from the liquid mixture you started with.

8. Share your treat with a friend or classmate!

Conclusions

▶ What made the liquid change to a solid?

▶ What name could you give your treat?

Follow-up

▶ Make another treat but use cream or canned milk instead of regular milk.

Changes in States

Matter can change from one state to another. A piece of chocolate left in a hot car melts. The solid chocolate changes to liquid chocolate. When you freeze fruit juice to make an ice pop, the liquid juice becomes a solid frozen dessert.

Solids and liquids

Heating a solid causes it to melt and become a liquid. Solids melt at different temperatures. Chocolate melts at about 36°C (96.8°F), which is just a little lower than your body temperature. That is why chocolate melts in your mouth or on your hands. Ice melts at 0°C (32°F).

Ice cream melts quickly on a summer day.

Some solids melt only at very high temperatures. Solid gold will not become liquid unless it is heated to a temperature of over 1,000°C. That is equal to almost 2,000°F!

It takes a very high temperature to melt gold.

Cooling a liquid can cause it to become a solid again. A candy maker melts chocolate and pours it into plastic molds. The liquid chocolate cools and becomes a solid again. When the plastic molds are taken off, the solid chocolate has the shape of the mold.

Candy can be heated and cooled to form fun shapes.

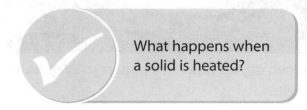

What happens when a solid is heated?

Liquids and gases

Solids can change to liquids, and liquids can change to solids. Liquids can also change another way. They can change to gases. Liquids become gases when they are heated enough.

Boiling water in a teakettle changes liquid water to a gas.

You have seen this happen when water boils in a pot or teakettle. The boiling water bubbles. Steam rises from the water. The steam is a gas. The gas is called water vapor. As the water vapor spreads out in the room, it seems to disappear, but it is still there.

Water vapor forms from boiling water, but it also forms as the sun warms bodies of water. The sun's heat causes the water in lakes, ponds, and even mud puddles to change to water vapor. When a liquid changes to a gas, the process is called **evaporation**. The water that evaporates stays in the air for a while.

The sun causes water in a puddle to evaporate.

When a gas changes to a liquid, the process is called **condensation**. This happens as water vapor in the air cools. Water vapor in the sky condenses and forms clouds. You can also see water vapor condense when you pour a cold drink into a glass on a hot day. Little drops of water form on the outside of the glass. The cold drink cools the glass and the air around it. The water vapor in the air condenses, or changes from a gas to a liquid.

Water vapor in the air condenses on the outside of a cool glass.

When does evaporation happen?

What is it called when a gas changes to a liquid?

Water

Any substance can change to another state, but most do not change easily. Most stay in the state we usually see them in. Iron is a solid. Gasoline is a liquid. Oxygen is a gas.

Water is different. It can easily change from one state to another. We see water most often in its liquid state, but ice, frost, and snow are solid forms of water. You cannot see the water vapor in the air, but it is water as a gas.

The Celsius temperature scale is based on the changing states of water. At 0°C water freezes and changes to a solid. At 100°C water boils and changes to a gas.

Most types of matter contract, or shrink, as they freeze. Water is one of the few kinds of matter that does not. Liquid water expands when it freezes. Frozen water, or ice, takes up more room than liquid water does.

Pour some water into a tall, clear plastic cup. Place the cup on a level surface and mark the level of the water. Put the cup in a freezer. Leave it there until the liquid becomes solid. Compare the level of the solid with the mark on the cup.

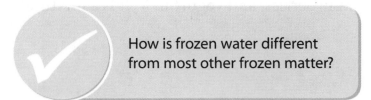

How is frozen water different
from most other frozen matter?

Changes in Matter

Matter can change in many ways. Its physical properties, such as color and shape, can change. It can change from one state to another. It can also combine with other matter to form new substances. All changes to matter are either physical changes or chemical changes.

Physical Changes

A **physical change** is a change in matter that does not form a new substance. If you have a cake to share with friends, you cut it into pieces. The pieces are still cake, just smaller pieces. The cake did not change into something new, but its size changed. If you put all the pieces together, they would have the same mass as the whole cake did.

Physical changes also happen when matter changes states. Ice cream straight from a freezer has a definite shape. It is a solid. When it melts, it changes to a liquid. The melted ice cream takes the shape of the bowl or container it is in. The ice cream has had a physical change, but it is still ice cream.

Physical changes can also happen when matter is mixed together. A **mixture** is two or more kinds of matter that are mixed together. A smoothie might have bananas, strawberries, and yogurt in it. It is a mixture.

To make a smoothie, you first cut the large fruit into smaller pieces. Cutting the fruit does not change the type of matter. The banana is still a banana. The strawberry is still a strawberry. But the fruit has had a physical change. Its size changed.

After cutting the fruit, you put it in a blender. You also add the yogurt. Then you blend everything together to form a thick liquid. You cannot see the fruit, but you can still taste both the fruit and the yogurt. Blending the ingredients together did not make a new kind of matter.

The fruit and yogurt have had physical changes.

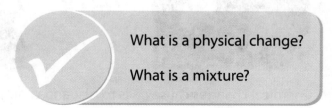

What is a physical change?

What is a mixture?

Chemical Changes

A **chemical change** is a change in matter that forms a new substance. Sometimes when we combine two or more kinds of matter, they form a new kind of matter. The different kinds of matter lose their own properties and take on new ones.

For example, to make brownies, you can use eggs, flour, sugar, cocoa, and butter. You blend those different kinds of matter together. When you bake the batter, the properties of the eggs, flour, sugar, cocoa, and butter change. The different kinds of matter combine and change to make a new kind of matter—brownie.

Another chemical change happens when iron rusts. Nails, garden tools, and other iron objects rust when they get wet. Water contains oxygen. The oxygen in the water mixes with the iron. When oxygen and iron combine, they form a new substance we call rust.

Chemical changes cause nails to rust and change brownie batter into a dessert.

Our Unchangeable God

Matter changes. God made it that way for our good. Allowing us to change matter is one way God provides for us. We make food, heat, shelter, and clothing from matter. Sometimes we change it from one state to another. We often cause physical and chemical changes. Because we can change matter, we can use it to meet our needs.

God, the Creator, does not change. He is always the same and will always keep His Word. Many verses in the Bible remind us that God cannot change. Psalm 102:25–27 describes how the earth and the heavens will change and perish but God will not. We can trust and depend on Him.

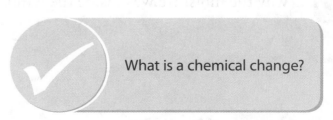

What is a chemical change?

Words to Know

matter
physical property
mass
volume
balance
gram

liter
graduated
  container
solid
liquid
gas

evaporation
condensation
physical change
mixture
chemical change

Key Ideas

▶ Matter has physical properties that can be observed and measured.

▶ Mass is measured in grams and kilograms.

▶ Volume is measured in liters and milliliters.

▶ Heating and cooling can cause matter to change from one state to another.

▶ The three states of water appear as ice, liquid water, and water vapor.

▶ Changes to matter are either physical or chemical changes.

Write About It

Maybe you have been in a warm car on a cold day and seen moisture on the window. Perhaps you even used your finger to draw pictures on the window. Write a paragraph explaining why the moisture was inside the window.

CHAPTER 6

Singing is a way to use sound to praise God. It is easy to sing when everything is going well. It is not so easy when things seem to be going wrong. The Bible tells us of a time when two Christians sang in prison. Paul and Silas had been preaching about Jesus. Some men thought they were causing trouble. The men beat Paul and Silas and threw them into prison. While in prison Paul and Silas prayed and began to sing. The other prisoners heard them. When God performed a miracle to set Paul and Silas free, they told the jailor about Jesus. He wanted to know the God they praised.

 Sound

Sound

Birds sing. Leaves rustle. Insects chirp. These sounds are just a few of the ones you might hear outside. Some sounds are noisy. Some sounds are quiet. The sounds in our world are a gift from God.

God gave us sounds to help us observe our world. Sounds can tell us about the things around us or warn us of danger. Other sounds are simply for us to enjoy.

Vibrations

Each sound you hear is caused by a moving object. The moving object causes vibrations. A **vibration** is a rapid back-and-forth movement. **Sound** is vibrations you can hear. You cannot see sound, but you may be able to see and feel the vibrations.

The source of a sound is a vibrating object. If you hit a bell, the bell starts to vibrate and causes a sound. You can feel that the bell is moving. If you touch the bell, you stop the vibrations. The sound from the bell also stops.

A tuning fork vibrates to produce a musical note.

What is sound?

Instruments

You can cause an object to vibrate by blowing on it, hitting it, plucking it, or rubbing it. Musicians use these actions to produce musical sounds. A trumpeter blows into a trumpet. The blowing causes the air inside the trumpet to vibrate. The top of a drum vibrates when it is hit. The strings of a guitar vibrate when they are plucked. A violinist rubs a bow across the strings of a violin to make the strings vibrate.

The sounds of your voice are also caused by vibrations. As air passes through your throat, your

blowing

hitting

108

vocal cords vibrate. These vibrations allow you to talk and sing. In the Bible, Psalm 150 tells of instruments that were used to worship God. Verse 6 of the psalm says "Let every thing that hath breath praise the Lord. Praise ye the Lord." Some people can play an instrument and make music to glorify God. You might not be able to play an instrument. But all of us can use the sounds our voices make to praise God.

plucking

rubbing

Singing is one way we can use our voices to praise God.

What are four ways you can make an object vibrate?

109

Sound Waves

What happens to the water when you drop a stone into a calm pond? Ripples, or waves, spread out from the place where the stone went into the water. The waves move outward.

Sound also travels in waves. A vibration causes sound waves. You cannot see the sound waves, but they act somewhat like the waves on the pond. The sound waves move outward from their source in all directions.

Because sound travels in all directions, the source of a sound does not need to be facing you for you to hear the sound. You can hear sounds beside, behind, and in front of you. You can also hear sounds above and below you.

Sound waves travel in all directions.

Sound and matter

Sounds that travel through the air may also travel through other forms of matter. You can sit in a room with the doors and windows closed. But you still might hear sounds from outside or from the next room. The sound travels through the air and then through the solid wall, door, or window.

Sound waves travel at different speeds through solids, liquids, and gases. Sound waves travel faster through liquids than through air. They travel the fastest through solids.

Speed of Sound

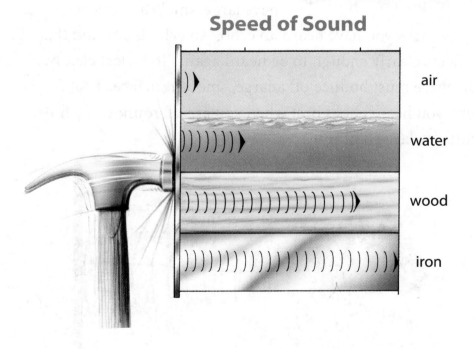

air

water

wood

iron

How does sound travel?

Through which kind of matter does sound travel the fastest?

Reflected sounds

Sound waves travel outward from a source. They keep moving outward until something blocks their path.

Sound reflects well in a canyon.

When a sound wave hits an object, the wave may bounce off it. We say the wave was reflected. Large, hard, smooth surfaces reflect sound waves better than other surfaces do. A large building or room might have these surfaces. Canyon walls also have large, smooth surfaces.

Perhaps you have heard an echo. An **echo** is a sound that reflects clearly enough to be heard again. To reflect clearly, the wave must bounce off a large, smooth surface. That is why you hear echoes best when you are surrounded by hills, cliffs, or large buildings.

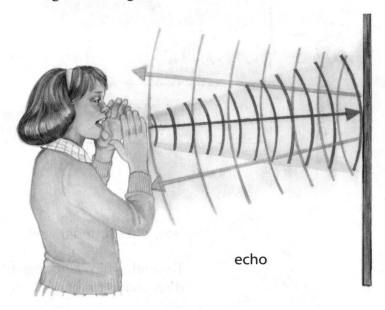
echo

Absorbed sounds

Sometimes sound waves are not reflected. They are absorbed. *Absorb* means "to take in." Rough or soft surfaces absorb sound. Uneven surfaces also absorb sound.

Some rooms can be very noisy. They have many hard, smooth surfaces. The walls, ceiling, and floor are all places that may reflect sound.

Materials that absorb sound can be used to make a room quieter. Rough, uneven materials can help keep sounds from being reflected. Carpet and ceiling tiles are materials used to absorb some of the sounds in a room.

Some materials absorb sound.

What kinds of surfaces reflect sound best?

What kinds of surfaces absorb sound?

The Ear and Hearing

The sense of hearing is located in the ears. The ears collect sound waves and send messages to the brain. This allows us to hear. The sound waves travel through the three main parts of the ear—the outer ear, the middle ear, and the inner ear.

The Outer Ear

When you think of your ear, you likely think of the part you can see on the side of your head. This is the outer ear. It includes the ear flap and the ear canal. The *ear flap* is the outside part of your ear that you can bend and pull. It protects the middle ear and collects sound waves.

The *ear canal* goes from the ear flap to the eardrum. It is shaped like a slightly curved tunnel. It is about 26 millimeters (1 in.) long. Sound waves travel through the ear canal to the eardrum. The sound waves cause the eardrum to vibrate.

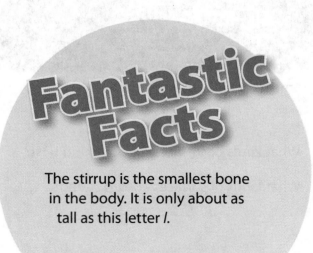

Fantastic Facts

The stirrup is the smallest bone in the body. It is only about as tall as this letter *l*.

Path of Sound

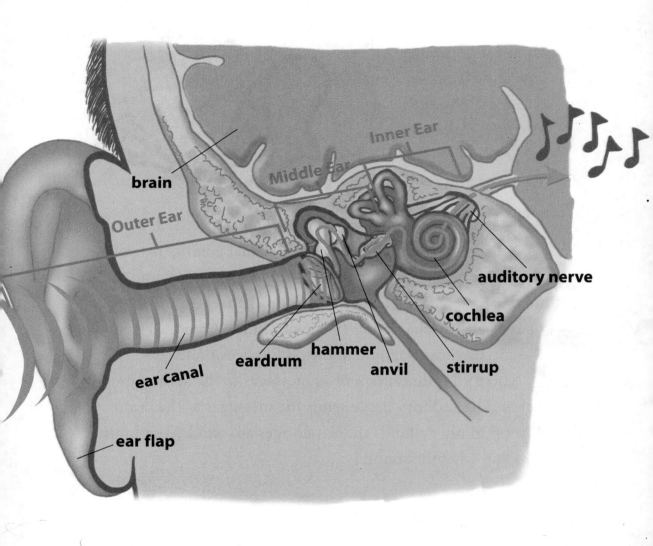

brain

Inner Ear

Middle Ear

Outer Ear

auditory nerve

cochlea

eardrum

hammer

anvil

stirrup

ear canal

ear flap

What are the three main parts of the ear?

The Middle Ear

The *eardrum* is a thin, tightly stretched membrane. As it vibrates, it causes three tiny bones in the middle ear to vibrate also. These three ear bones are called the *hammer*, the *anvil*, and the *stirrup*. These bones move the vibrations on to the inner ear.

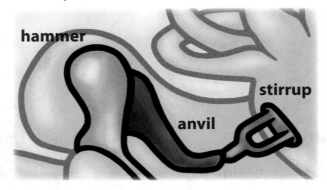

The Inner Ear

Behind the three small bones is a small opening that goes into the inner ear. The inner ear includes the *cochlea* and the *auditory nerve*. The cochlea is a chamber that is in the shape of a spiral. The chamber is filled with fluid. Vibrations from the stirrup cause the fluid in the cochlea to vibrate.

These vibrations are sent as messages to the auditory nerve. The auditory nerve sends the messages to the brain. The brain understands these messages as sound. Your brain tells you what the sound is.

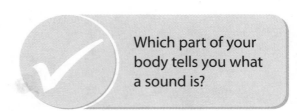

Which part of your body tells you what a sound is?

EXPLORATIONS

ALL EARS

Most of the time we think about the outside parts of our ears. How big are they? Are they clean? But the most important parts of our ears are inside our heads.

In this exploration you will build a model of the ear.

What to Do

1. Get a stiff piece of cardboard or foam board. Use a pencil to draw a diagram of the ear. Use the diagram on page 115 as a guide.

2. Your model should be more than just a drawing of the ear. You will need to choose materials to represent some of the parts for your model. For example, you might choose to use part of a balloon for the eardrum.

3. Assemble your model. Be sure the pieces will not fall off your board. Label the ear flap, ear canal, eardrum, hammer, anvil, stirrup, cochlea, and auditory nerve.

4. Share your model with others.

Characteristics of Sound

Pitch

Pitch is how high or low a sound is. Every sound has a pitch. Pitch depends on how fast the source of the sound is vibrating. A big bass has a low pitch. It has long strings, and they vibrate slowly. A small violin has a high pitch. The strings are shorter and vibrate faster.

A string player changes the pitch by moving the position of his fingers on the strings. When he makes the strings shorter, the instrument plays a higher pitch.

Volume

Volume is how loud or soft a sound is. When you shout to a friend from across a ball field, you make a loud sound. When you whisper a secret to your friend, you make a soft sound. Volume

Fantastic Facts

A mosquito beats its wings 300–600 times a second. The fast vibration of its wings causes the high buzzing sound you hear.

loud

soft

depends on how much force is used to make an object vibrate. When a stronger force is used, the vibration makes a louder sound. A weaker force makes a softer sound.

Sound waves spread out as they move farther away from the source of their vibrations. The vibrations become weaker. The sound becomes quieter.

Quality

The **quality** of a sound is what makes that sound different from all other sounds. Quality helps us identify different people's voices. It also helps us hear the differences between the sounds of different instruments. Even when a clarinet and a flute play the same note, they sound different.

clarinet

flute

✓ What is pitch?

What is volume?

Uses of Sounds

Some sounds are pleasing to us. Most people enjoy listening to good music. We like to hear the voices of our friends and family.

Other sounds are harmful. Loud, harsh sounds can damage our ears. That is why people who work with loud machines should wear ear protection.

We use sound to communicate to each other. We hear the sounds others make, and we make sounds for others to hear. The words we say are very important. The Bible tells us that our speech should please God. Psalm 19:14 says "Let the words of my mouth . . . be acceptable in thy sight, O Lord."

Speech is not the only way to communicate. Other sounds can communicate as well. A ringing alarm clock tells you it is time to get up. A stove timer buzzes when it is time to take something out of the oven. A siren on a police car, a fire truck, or an ambulance warns drivers to move out of the way.

In Bible times the sound of trumpets was often used to communicate information. The priests blew trumpets to tell the people to gather in one place. Trumpets were often used in the worship services at the temple as well. In times of war trumpets were used to send men into battle.

God has given us the wonderful gift of sound. He wants us to use that gift in a way that honors Him. The sounds we choose to make should help others hear about what a great God we have.

Name some sounds used to communicate.

Musical Bottles

The pitch of an instrument is related to the length of the vibrating part. Long strings make low sounds. Short strings make high sounds. Some instruments, such as trumpets, control the amount of air that vibrates. This gives those instruments a high or low pitch.

In this activity you will find out how the amount of vibrating air affects pitch.

Problem

How does the amount of air in a bottle affect its pitch?

Materials
2 plastic bottles, 20 oz
800 mL water
metric measuring cups
funnel
Activity Manual

Procedure

1. Complete the hypothesis in your Activity Manual.
2. Label one bottle *A* and the other *B*.
3. Measure 100 mL of water. Use a funnel to pour the water into bottle A.
4. Measure 300 mL of water. Use a funnel to pour the water into bottle B.
5. Gently blow across the top of each bottle. Listen carefully to the pitch of the sound.

6. Decide which bottle has the higher pitch. Record your observation.

122

7. Measure 400 mL of water.

8. Use a funnel to pour that water into bottle A. Bottle A should now have 500 mL of water.

9. Blow across the top of the bottles again. Listen to the sounds.

 10. Record your observation.

Conclusions

▶ How does the amount of vibrating air affect the pitch?

▶ How could you change the pitch of the sound?

Follow-up

▶ Repeat the activity but use larger bottles.

▶ Fill eight bottles with different amounts of water to try to make a musical scale.

Words to Know

vibration	echo	volume
sound	pitch	quality

Key Ideas

▶ Sound is vibrations you can hear.

▶ Vibrations can be made by blowing, hitting, plucking, or rubbing an object.

▶ Sound travels in waves. These waves move outward from their source in all directions.

▶ Sound waves travel at different speeds through solids, liquids, and gases.

▶ Large, hard, smooth surfaces reflect sound waves. Rough, soft, or uneven surfaces absorb sound waves.

▶ The three main parts of the ear are the outer ear, middle ear, and inner ear. Sound passes from the outer ear through the middle ear to the inner ear, which sends messages to the brain.

▶ The stronger the vibration is, the louder the sound is. Sounds get quieter as they move away from the source.

Write About It

In a set of handbells there are some very small bells and some very large bells. Explain which bells have higher pitches and why.

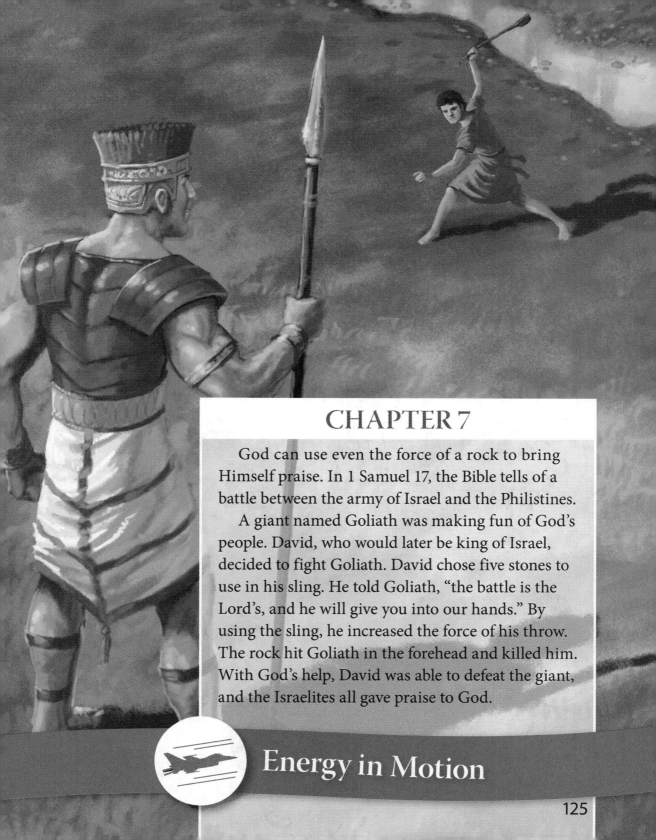

CHAPTER 7

God can use even the force of a rock to bring Himself praise. In 1 Samuel 17, the Bible tells of a battle between the army of Israel and the Philistines.

A giant named Goliath was making fun of God's people. David, who would later be king of Israel, decided to fight Goliath. David chose five stones to use in his sling. He told Goliath, "the battle is the Lord's, and he will give you into our hands." By using the sling, he increased the force of his throw. The rock hit Goliath in the forehead and killed him. With God's help, David was able to defeat the giant, and the Israelites all gave praise to God.

Energy in Motion

Force

Think about what happens when you want to sit down at a table. If the chairs are pushed up against the table, you have to pull a chair out so you can sit on it. After you get up, you push the chair back against the table. You use a force to move the chair.

A **force** is a push or pull. You use a force to kick a ball. You also use force to turn a jump rope. Objects cannot move unless a force causes them to move.

Force also affects objects that are already moving. Force is what makes objects go faster, slow down, or change direction. Think about a merry-go-round. Using force, you can make the merry-go-round go faster, go slower, or change its direction.

When you kick a soccer ball, you put a force on the ball. The ball goes in the same direction as the force. An object will move in the same direction as the force that moves it.

You may pass the ball to someone else on your team. Your teammate kicks the ball in another direction. When the direction of the force changes, the direction of the ball changes.

You swing a jump rope around in a circle for your friends to jump over. The force of your swing keeps the rope turning until another force stops it.

What is force?

What makes objects move?

Invisible Forces

When you kick a ball you can clearly see the force that causes the ball to move. The force puts the ball in motion or changes the direction of the motion. But your kick is not the only force affecting the ball. There are other forces at work as well.

Even if no one stops the ball, at some point it will stop rolling. A force called friction is working on the ball. **Friction** is a force that slows or stops motion. As the ball rolls across the ground, friction causes it to slow down and stop.

Friction causes a sled to slow down and stop.

Gravity causes the water in a fountain to fall back to the earth.

If you kick the ball up into the air, it does not keep going up forever. It falls back down. An invisible force called gravity pulls the ball down. **Gravity** is the force that pulls objects toward the center of the earth.

When you weigh an object, you are measuring the pull of gravity. **Weight** is the amount of force gravity has on an object. You can use a scale to measure how much force gravity has on that object. Weight and mass are not the same. The mass of an object is how much matter is in the object.

If you have ever played with a magnet, you have seen another invisible force at work. The force of a magnet is called **magnetism**. A magnet does not have to touch an object to put a force on it. Think of using a magnet to pick up a paper clip. You hold the magnet over the paper clip. Suddenly the magnetic force pulls the paper clip up to the magnet.

Magnetism pulls paper clips toward a magnet.

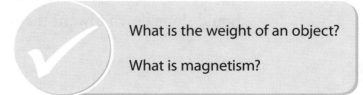

What is the weight of an object?

What is magnetism?

Friction Fun

Though we do not think about it, friction greatly affects our lives. Depending on what we are doing, we may need more friction or less friction. A baseball player does not want to slide and fall when he is trying to catch a ball. Shoes with cleats provide more friction and help him keep from slipping. Skiers put wax on the bottom of their skis. The wax decreases the friction and helps the skis glide quickly on the snow.

In this activity you will test some surfaces to find out which one has the most friction.

Problem

Which surface has the most friction?

Procedure

1. Complete the hypothesis in your Activity Manual.
2. Lay the towel on the floor. Smooth out all the wrinkles. Lay the notebook on one end of the towel. The "ramp" should slope down toward the middle of the towel.

Materials
3-ring notebook, 1 in.
golf ball
centimeter ruler
large towel
pan of sand
carpet
Activity Manual

3. Hold the golf ball at the top of the ramp. Release the ball and let it roll down the ramp and onto the towel.

4. Use the ruler to measure the distance from the edge of the notebook to where the ball stopped. Record the distance.

5. Repeat steps 3–4 with the sand and carpet. Measure and record the distance each time.

Conclusions

▶ How can you tell which surface has the most friction?

▶ Was your hypothesis correct?

Follow-up

▶ Repeat the activity but use other surfaces.

Motion

In a baseball game, the pitcher throws the ball toward home plate. The batter hits the ball. He puts a force on the ball. The force sets the ball in motion. **Motion** is a change of position.

To measure how much an object moves, you must have a starting point. When you have a starting point, you can describe the motion of an object in three ways. You can tell what direction the object travels, how far it travels, and how fast it travels.

When batting in a baseball game, the starting point is home plate. From home plate a baseball can go many directions. It might go left over third base or right toward first base. It might even go behind the batter. You can describe the direction the ball moves from home plate.

You can also measure how far a ball travels from home plate. It might go far into the outfield. Or it may go only a few meters in front of home plate. If you measure from where the ball starts to where it stops, you can tell how far it travels.

You can also tell how fast a ball travels. If a ball slowly rolls to the first baseman, he can easily pick it up. But if a ball quickly whizzes into the outfield, a player may not be able to get there fast enough to catch it.

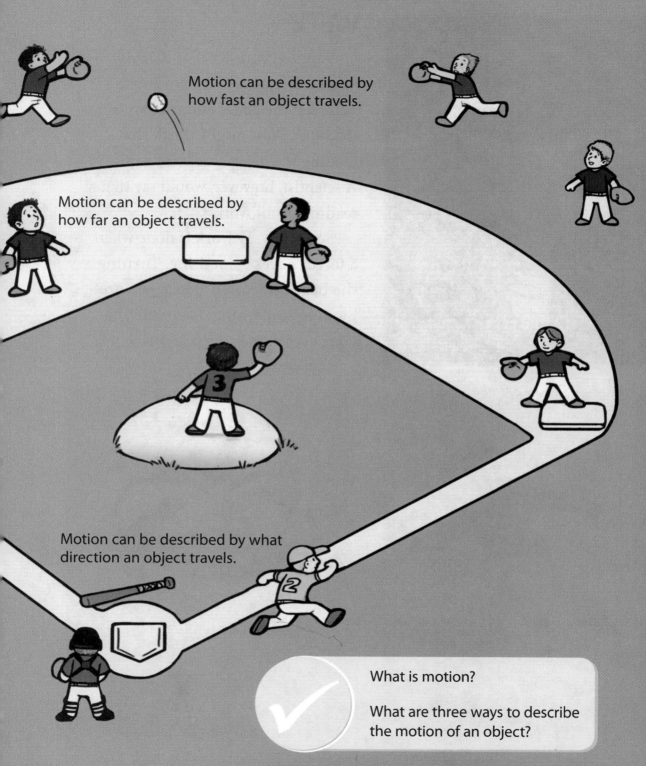

Motion can be described by how fast an object travels.

Motion can be described by how far an object travels.

Motion can be described by what direction an object travels.

What is motion?

What are three ways to describe the motion of an object?

133

Work

Suppose your teacher told you to read five pages in your book. You read the pages and put down the book. You might think that reading the pages was hard work. A scientist, however, would say that reading is not work.

Scientists say **work** is done when a force moves something. Turning the pages is work because you are moving something. Even moving your eyes across the pages is work.

But understanding the text is not work. You are not moving anything.

If you carry some books across the room, you are doing work. If you just hold the books, you are not doing work. Nothing is moving.

Sometimes other forces do work. If you drop the books, you do not apply a force but work is still done. The force of gravity causes the books to move.

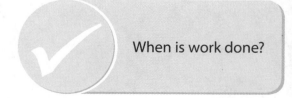

When is work done?

Measuring Work

You do work when you use a force to move something a distance. To know how much work is done, you measure how much force pushes or pulls an object and how far the object moves. Work is measured by the amount of force times the distance.

force × distance = work

Doing Work

People can do work. You work when you move yourself or some object. Animals work by carrying loads for us. They also pull and drag things.

People and animals are not the only ones who do work, though. Wind and moving water can also do work. Wind works when it moves windmills, flags, or leaves. Flowing water moves logs, rocks, boats, and water wheels.

Machines do a lot of work. Cars, trucks, tractors, and airplanes move people and things every day.

People try to find better ways to get work done. Simple machines are the basic tools that make work easier. They do not decrease the amount of work, and they cannot do work on their own. Something else must supply the force. But these tools do make work easier.

lever

wheel and axle

inclined plane

How is work measured?

Name three things that can do work.

Energy

You use energy every day. When you get out of bed, you use energy. When you play on the playground, you use energy. Even opening a book uses energy. **Energy** is the ability to do work.

When you are playing or a car is running, it is easy to see that energy is being used. Some things, though, have energy that is not being used. These things have stored energy. Stored energy can be used later to do work.

You have probably had a toy that needed batteries. Without the batteries, the toy did not do the work that it was made to do. Batteries have stored energy. Other objects use the stored energy to work.

Food has stored energy. We eat food to get energy. We use the energy to do work.

Another kind of stored energy is fuel. Gasoline is a fuel.

Drivers put gasoline into cars to provide energy to make the car run.

Batteries, food, and fuel are all examples of things that have stored energy. They have energy that can be changed into a form of work.

stored energy

Science and the Bible

In Bible times, there were no flashlights. Instead people carried small lamps for light. The lamps used olive oil to produce light. The oil provided the stored energy needed for the light. In Psalm 119:105 the Bible says, "Thy word is a lamp unto my feet, and a light unto my path." Just as a lamp gives light in the darkness, the Word of God shows us how to live in a world full of sin.

What is energy?

Name something that has stored energy.

Kinds of Energy

There are many kinds of energy. Sound and light are two kinds of energy. Light from the sun provides the energy for plants to make food.

Electrical energy is another kind of energy. We use it to light our homes. We use it for cooking and heating. We also use electrical energy to power our computers.

Most machines have mechanical energy. Mechanical energy is the energy caused by an object's motion or position. When you ride your bicycle you move the pedals. The motion is mechanical energy. Coasting down a hill is also mechanical energy. You do not provide the energy. The position of the bike at the top of the hill allows you to go down the hill.

Chemical energy comes from burning fuels, such as burning gasoline in a car. It also comes from the food that we eat.

Changes to Energy

Energy can change from one form to another. A plant uses light energy to make food. The light energy is stored by the plant as chemical energy.

light energy   **chemical energy**   **mechanical energy**

A person eats the food. The person uses the chemical energy from the food to produce mechanical energy.

In a flashlight the chemical energy in the batteries changes to electrical energy. The electrical energy heats the wire in the light bulb. Heat makes the wire glow, and you can see the light energy.

God has allowed man to make many things that help people work. But God is still the giver of all the things that we have. In 1 Timothy 6:17 the Bible says, "Charge them that are rich in this world, that they be not highminded, nor trust in uncertain riches, but in the living God, who giveth us richly all things to enjoy." We should thank God for the abilities that He has given us.

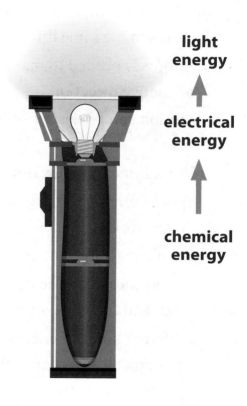

light energy

↑

electrical energy

↑

chemical energy

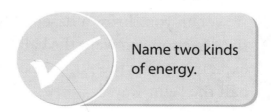

Name two kinds of energy.

Words to Know

force	gravity	magnetism	work
friction	weight	motion	energy

Key Ideas

▶ An object cannot move unless a force moves it. The object moves in the same direction as the force that moves it.

▶ A force is needed to make an object go faster, slow down, or change direction.

▶ Motion can be described by its direction, distance, and speed.

▶ Work is measured by multiplying the force by the distance.

▶ People, animals, wind, moving water, and machines can all do work.

▶ Simple machines make work easier.

▶ Stored energy can be used later to do work. Batteries, food, and fuel have stored energy.

▶ Different kinds of energy include light, sound, electrical, mechanical, and chemical. Energy can be changed from one form to another.

Write About It

When you throw a baseball, your arm should point in the direction you want the ball to go. Write a few sentences explaining why the position of your arm can help send the ball the right way.

4 God's Earth and Sky

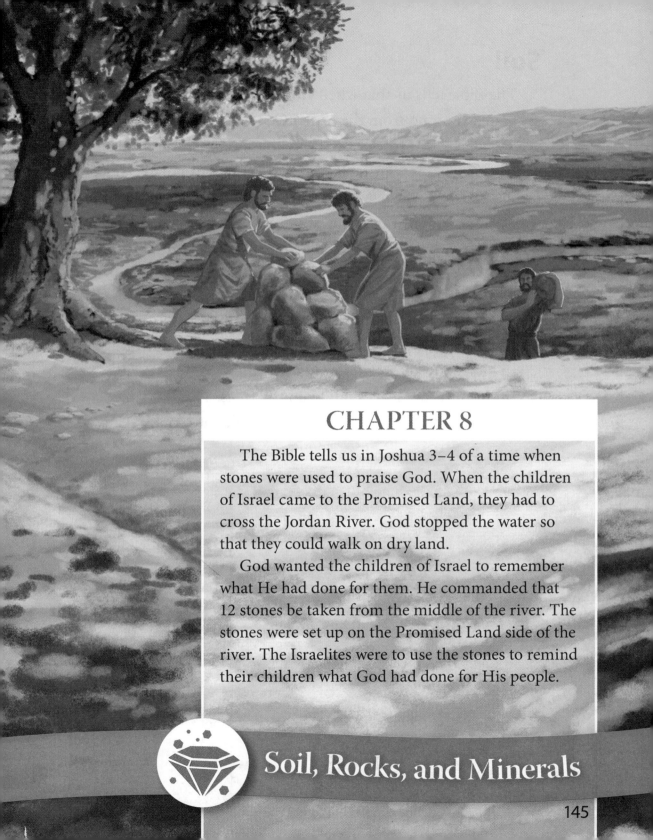

CHAPTER 8

The Bible tells us in Joshua 3–4 of a time when stones were used to praise God. When the children of Israel came to the Promised Land, they had to cross the Jordan River. God stopped the water so that they could walk on dry land.

God wanted the children of Israel to remember what He had done for them. He commanded that 12 stones be taken from the middle of the river. The stones were set up on the Promised Land side of the river. The Israelites were to use the stones to remind their children what God had done for His people.

Soil, Rocks, and Minerals

Soil

The Bible tells us that when God created the world He separated the land from the water (Genesis 1:9–10). The land is a wonderful gift from God. It provides many things for us.

Another name for dirt is *soil*. **Soil** is the loose material on the earth's surface. Many living things depend on the soil. Some animals live in the soil. Most plants need soil to grow, and both animals and people need plants for food.

Parts of Soil

If you pick up a handful of soil, you might see tiny pieces of rock. You will see other things as well. Soil is made of small bits of broken rock, humus, air, and water.

In the autumn, leaves fall from the trees. They become brown and dry. After a while they crumble into small

pieces. The leaves seem to just disappear, but they do not. Over time the remains of the leaves become part of the humus in the soil. **Humus** is the remains of living things that have died and decayed. Plants and animals decay, or break down, after they die. After a while they become part of the soil.

Soil contains water and air as well as humus. Water is stored in the soil. There are also tiny spaces of air in the soil. To grow well, plants need both water and spaces of air.

Not all plants need the same amounts of humus, water, and air. God has made the world with many kinds of soil so that many different kinds of plants can grow.

What is soil made of?

What is humus?

Layers of Soil

Soil forms in layers. Most of the time we see only the top layer. This layer is called topsoil. **Topsoil** is the layer that contains humus. Plants grow in this layer.

Under the topsoil is another layer. It is called **subsoil**. The subsoil layer does not contain humus. This layer has larger pieces of rock in it than the topsoil does.

Large, unbroken rock lies under the subsoil. It is called **bedrock**.

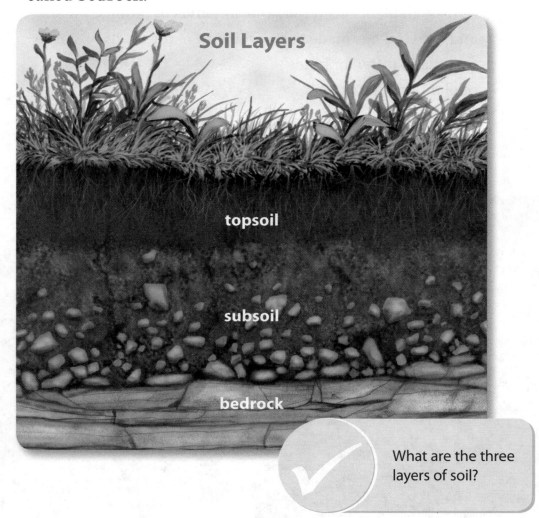

Soil Layers

topsoil

subsoil

bedrock

What are the three layers of soil?

Dirt Cup

Would you like to eat dirt for lunch? Earthworms do. But people and most animals do not eat dirt. In this activity you will make a model of the layers of the soil. This "dirt" you will like to eat!

Materials
1 clear plastic cup, 9 oz
1 whole cookie
1 cup of pudding
spoon
1 broken cookie
1 crushed cookie
Activity Manual

Purpose

Model the layers of soil.

Procedure

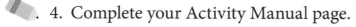

1. Place the whole cookie in the bottom of the empty cup.
2. Spoon half the pudding on top of the cookie. Add the broken cookie and stir.
3. Stir the crushed cookie into the leftover pudding. Spoon the mixture on top of the broken-cookie layer.
4. Complete your Activity Manual page.

Conclusions

▶ Which layer of pudding represents subsoil?

Follow-up

▶ Use different materials to make another model of the layers of the soil.

Weathering

God designed the surface of our earth so that it is always changing. Rocks, even huge ones, are slowly broken into smaller pieces. These little pieces become part of the soil and replace the soil that is used by man.

What causes rocks to break apart? Water, ice, wind, and plants can change rocks. They can cause rocks to break apart. The breaking down of rocks is called **weathering**.

Water and Wind

Flowing water weathers rocks. The water in a stream moves over and around the rocks. The water slowly wears away the rocks and smoothes them. Rocks are also carried by the water. As the stream tumbles the rocks, the water wears away any sharp edges. The water carries away the bits. The worn rocks are rounded and smooth.

Wind weathers rocks in somewhat the same way. The wind blows sand against rocks. The sand rubs the surfaces of the rocks. Over time this wears away bits of the rocks and smoothes them.

Rocks weathered by water are rounded and smooth.

Ice and Plants

Flowing water and wind smooth rocks by breaking off small bits, but other forces can break rocks into pieces. When water flows into the cracks of a rock and freezes, it becomes ice. The ice takes up more space than the flowing water did. The ice pushes the rock apart. As the rock is forced apart, it breaks into pieces.

Plants can also weather rocks. Over time even a tiny plant can break a strong rock. A seed can fall into a small crack in a rock. As a plant grows from the seed and gets bigger, it pushes with great force. It makes the crack wider and wider. The plant can break the rock into pieces.

As a plant grows, it can break a rock.

What is the breaking down of rocks called?

What are four things that can weather rocks?

Rocks

Perhaps you have dug up rocks in a garden or walked on large rocks in a stream. **Rocks** are hard pieces of the earth's surface. They are many sizes and shapes. Some are small and can easily be picked up. Others are larger and heavier than you can lift. A rock might be as big as a car or even a tall building. Some rocks are as big as mountains.

Though rocks come in many shapes and sizes, scientists classify them into three groups. The three groups are igneous, sedimentary, and metamorphic. Rocks are classified by how they are formed.

Igneous Rock

Igneous rock forms when hot, melted rock cools. The melted rock comes from deep in the earth. There the rock is a very hot liquid.

A **volcano** is an opening in the earth that allows melted rock to come to the surface. Sometimes the melted rock may erupt, or come out quickly.

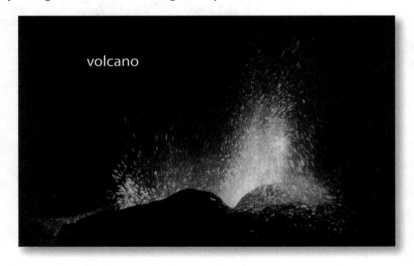

volcano

obsidian

granite

The melted rock cools and hardens. Some melted rock cools quickly. It forms rocks that are smooth. Obsidian is a smooth igneous rock. It is so smooth that it looks like glass.

Granite is a common igneous rock. It forms when melted rock cools slowly. This rock is often speckled. It may have shiny crystal spots. Granite has a rough surface instead of a smooth surface. Some mountains are made of granite.

✓

What are rocks?

What is igneous rock formed from?

Science and History

Mount Rushmore is a famous granite mountain in South Dakota. Huge faces of four United States presidents have been carved in the side of this mountain.

Sedimentary Rock

When rocks are weathered, the pieces often are moved from one place to another by water. The pieces that drop and fall to the bottom of the water are called sediment. The water presses down on the sediment. **Sedimentary rock** forms when layers of sediment are pressed together and harden.

sandstone

Because it is made of layers, sedimentary rock often has a striped look.

There are many different kinds of sedimentary rock. One kind is limestone. It forms from the shells and bones of sea animals. The shells and bones break apart after the animals die. When pressed together, the bits of shell and bone form limestone.

Sandstone is a rock that is made when layers of sand get pressed together. Shale forms from layers of mud.

Sometimes fossils are found in sedimentary rock. A **fossil** is any part or mark of a living thing that is naturally preserved after it dies. Most fossils formed during the Flood. At that time living things were buried very quickly.

fossil

Metamorphic Rock

The third kind of rock is metamorphic rock. The word *metamorphic* comes from the same word that *metamorphosis* does. It means "to change." **Metamorphic rock** forms when igneous or sedimentary rocks are changed by great heat and pressure.

Limestone is a soft sedimentary rock. But after it is placed under heat and pressure, it becomes marble. Artists often use marble because of its beauty and hardness.

Shale can change into a rock called slate. Slate can be split into thin sheets. Landscapers use it for some walkways and yard decorations. It is also used as a material for roofs.

Granite can change into a rock called gneiss. Gneiss is strong and often used as a building material.

marble statue

Rocks are always changing. Big rocks break into smaller rocks. Melted rock changes to solid rock. One kind of rock becomes another. These changes are called the rock cycle.

What kind of rock forms when layers of sediment are pressed together?

What kind of rock forms when other rocks are changed by great heat and pressure?

Minerals

Pirates sometimes had treasures of gold and silver. Their treasure was sparkling and shiny. Gold and silver are valuable treasures, but not all treasure sparkles and shines.

The rocks around us have many valuable treasures. Rocks are made of one or more minerals. **Minerals** are solid materials in nature that were never alive. The earth's minerals are a great treasure to us.

Uses of Minerals

We use minerals in many ways. You probably have eaten some minerals today. Many breakfast cereals contain iron. Iron is a mineral that your body needs to work properly. Calcium is another mineral you need. Milk is a good source of calcium.

Some minerals are hard to find or hard to get for use. Because of this, they are called precious metals. Gold and silver are two precious metals. Other minerals are cut and polished to reflect light. These minerals are called gems. Precious metals and gems are often used in jewelry.

Other minerals are easier to find. We say they are common minerals. Halite, graphite, and quartz are some common minerals. We get salt from the mineral halite. The "lead" in our pencils is not really lead at all. It is really a mix of clay and the mineral graphite. Quartz is probably the most common of all the minerals. Most sand is made of tiny bits of quartz. It is an important mineral used to make glass. Quartz is also used in computers and cell phones.

gold

graphite

quartz

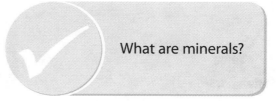

What are minerals?

Characteristics of Minerals

Minerals are not all alike. Some are hard, and some are soft. Scientists can test how hard or soft a mineral is. This is one way they can identify the mineral. A scientist named Friedrich Mohs studied some minerals. He put them in order from softest to hardest. His arrangement formed a scale. Other minerals can be compared to the scale that Mohs made.

A scratch test may be done to find out how hard a mineral is. A harder mineral can scratch a softer one. The hardness of a mineral is shown by what it can or cannot scratch.

Talc is a very soft mineral. It is used to make a soft powder. Almost every other mineral can scratch talc. Diamonds are very hard. They can cut, or scratch, all other minerals. Diamonds are used in jewelry. But they are also used in drills and other tools that cut hard things.

Mohs Scale

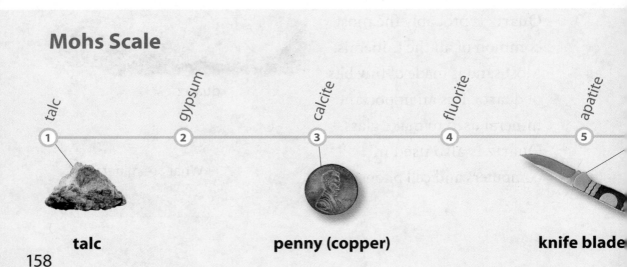

| 1 | 2 | 3 | 4 | 5 |

talc · gypsum · calcite · fluorite · apatite

talc   penny (copper)   knife blade

Most minerals form crystals. Each mineral has its own crystal shape. Scientists can use the shape of a crystal to help them know what mineral it is.

Minerals are different colors, but the colors of some minerals look alike. Scientists may use a streak test to help them identify a mineral. They rub the mineral on a white tile. The color of the mark it makes on the tile helps them know what mineral it is.

Gold and pyrite look alike. They are both yellow, but a streak test can be used to tell them apart. Gold leaves a yellowish streak. Pyrite leaves a green streak.

Salt crystals look like little boxes.

The dark streak shows this is pyrite, not gold.

What are two mineral characteristics that scientists can use to help tell minerals apart?

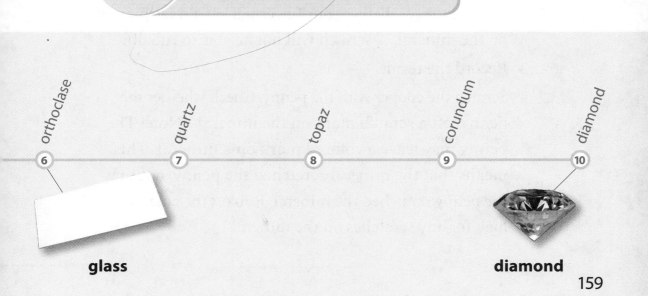

orthoclase
6

quartz
7

topaz
8

corundum
9

diamond
10

glass

diamond

ACTIVITY

Hard or Soft

Many soft things also scratch easily. Some minerals are soft. They can be scratched easily. Other minerals are more difficult to scratch.

In this activity you will test the hardness of several minerals.

Materials

penny
steel nail
copper
gypsum
quartz
zinc
Activity Manual

Problem

Which minerals can be scratched with each tool?

Procedure

1. Predict whether each tool (fingernail, penny, or nail) can scratch the copper. Record your predictions in your Activity Manual.

2. Scratch the copper with your fingernail. Look at the mineral to see whether your fingernail left a scratch mark on the mineral. A scratch will not be able to rub off.

3. Record the result.

4. Scratch the copper with the penny. Check whether the penny left a scratch mark on the mineral. (Note: The penny may leave a colored mark on a mineral. This means that the mineral scratched the penny, not that the penny scratched the mineral. Rub off the color and look for any scratches on the mineral.)

5. Record the result.

6. Scratch the copper with the nail. Check whether the nail left a scratch mark on the mineral.

7. Record the result.

8. Repeat the procedure for each mineral.

Conclusions

▶ Which mineral(s) can be scratched with your fingernail?

▶ Which mineral is the hardest?

Follow-up

▶ Make your own hardness scale. Arrange your minerals from softest to hardest.

Words to Know

soil	weathering	fossil
humus	rock	metamorphic rock
topsoil	igneous rock	mineral
subsoil	volcano	
bedrock	sedimentary rock	

Key Ideas

▶ Soil is made of small bits of broken rock, humus, air, and water.

▶ Topsoil, subsoil, and bedrock are the three main layers of soil.

▶ The surface of the earth is always changing.

▶ Water, ice, wind, and plants can weather rocks.

▶ Water and wind break small bits off rocks. Ice and plants can break rocks into pieces.

▶ Obsidian and granite are igneous rocks. Limestone is a sedimentary rock. Marble is a metamorphic rock.

▶ Rocks are made of one or more minerals.

▶ We use minerals in many ways.

▶ Minerals are identified by characteristics such as hardness, crystal shape, color, and streak.

Write About It

A farmer plants crops in an area that was once covered with trees. He expects crops to grow well in the area. Explain why he thinks the soil will be good for growing crops.

CHAPTER 9

God often uses weather to show His power. In Jonah 1 the Bible tells of how God controlled a storm so that men would praise Him.

Jonah was a prophet who did not want to go where God had told him to go. He got in a ship and tried to run away, but God caused a terrible storm to come. The ship was in danger of sinking, and the sailors were afraid. Jonah told the sailors that God had sent the storm because of him. He told them to throw him into the sea. When they did, the storm stopped. The sailors offered a sacrifice to God. They knew He had power over the storm.

Weather

Wind blows. Rain falls. Lightning flashes. Thunder booms! Often we think of these events when we think of weather. But weather is also clear skies, pleasant breezes, warm days, and cool nights. **Weather** is the condition of the air at a certain time and place.

All our weather takes place in the atmosphere. The **atmosphere** is a blanket of air that surrounds the earth. The atmosphere is a thin layer, but it is very important to us. God planned it to help protect the earth. The atmosphere helps keep the temperatures on the earth from being too hot or too cold for us to live.

atmosphere (air)

Measuring the Weather

The weather affects many things we do. You might carry an umbrella if it is going to rain. You put on a coat, gloves, and a hat if it is very cold. You may not be able to have an outdoor event because of stormy weather.

Temperature

One thing we often ask about weather is "What is the temperature?" The temperature is the measure of how hot or cold something is. When we measure the temperature for the weather, we are measuring how hot or cold the air is.

thermometer with degree markings

A thermometer is used to measure temperature. There are different kinds of thermometers. On some thermometers we read the degree markings to find the temperature. Many thermometers used for weather are digital. They show the temperature on a display.

digital thermometer

What is weather?

What do we use to measure the temperature of the air?

Precipitation

Another part of weather is precipitation. **Precipitation** is water that falls from the sky to the ground. Rain, snow, sleet, and hail are all forms of precipitation.

Rain is a liquid. It can fall only if the air temperature is above freezing. Rain falls all over the earth. It falls on

rain

the ground and in the ocean and other bodies of water. It provides water for all living things. In Hebrews 6:7 the Bible tells us the earth soaks up the rain that falls and plants grow. God gives the blessing of rain so that plants can grow.

Scientists use a **rain gauge** to measure rainfall. Each day they record how much rain fell. To find out what the normal rainfall for an area is, they collect measurements for a long time. They use the information, or data, to look for patterns. The patterns show what the normal rainfall is and when it occurs.

Places such as tropical rainforests receive a lot of rain. Other places, such as deserts, get very little rain. Sometimes an area does not

rain gauge

receive as much precipitation as it needs. When this happens, the lack of precipitation is called a drought. A drought can cause plants to die.

When parts of the air are below freezing, precipitation may fall as a form of ice. Snow, sleet, and hail form when water freezes before it reaches the ground. Snow and sleet occur in cold weather. Hail sometimes forms in thunderstorm clouds.

snow

What is used to measure rain?

What are three kinds of precipitation?

The water cycle

Water falls from the sky. It soaks into the ground or falls into a body of water. Precipitation is part of a cycle that moves water from the sky to the earth and back again. This movement of water is called the water cycle. God placed exactly the right amount of water on the earth for people, animals, and plants. As water goes through the water cycle, it is used again and again.

For the water cycle to occur, water must get back into the air. This part of the water cycle is called *evaporation*. When water heats up, it changes from a liquid to a gas. The gas that forms is called water vapor.

The warm water vapor rises in the atmosphere. As the water vapor rises, the temperature of the air gets colder. This cools the water vapor. Cool water vapor changes to a liquid. This is called *condensation*. The condensed water vapor forms clouds. A cloud grows as more and more water vapor condenses.

The droplets of water vapor attach to each other to form raindrops. When the drops become heavy, they fall to the ground as *precipitation*.

What gas forms when water evaporates?

What do we call the change from a gas (vapor) to a liquid?

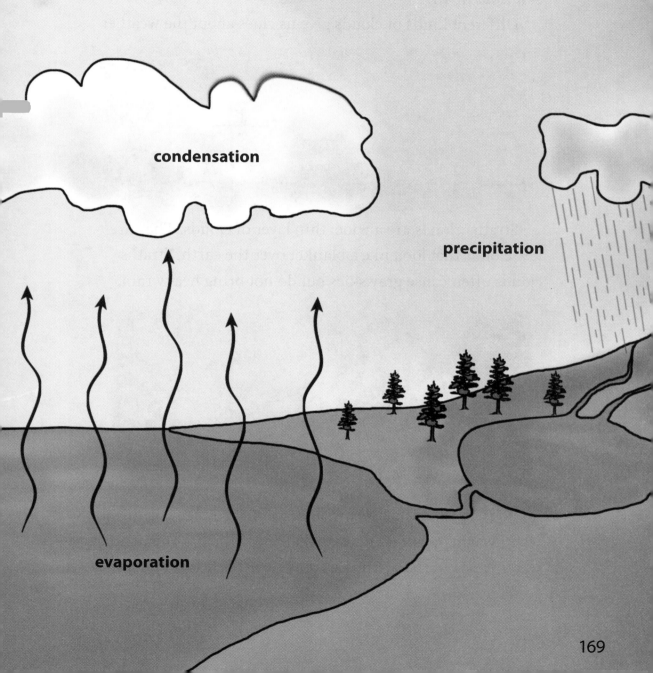

Water Cycle

condensation

precipitation

evaporation

Clouds

When water vapor condenses, it forms clouds. A cloud is a collection of very tiny water droplets or ice crystals. The droplets and crystals are so small and light that they can float in air.

Different kinds of clouds give us clues about the weather.

Stratus clouds are a wide, thin layer of clouds. They are low clouds that look like a blanket over the earth. Stratus clouds often cause gray skies but do not bring heavy rain.

Fog is a cloud that forms close to the ground. Fog forms when warm air blows over cold air near the ground. The water vapor in the warm air cools close to the ground and condenses.

Cumulus clouds are fluffy, cottonlike clouds. They usually mean the weather is fair, but these clouds can grow large and tall and form thunderclouds. The dark gray thunderclouds can bring stormy weather. The storms can have strong winds and heavy rain.

Cirrus clouds are high, thin, wispy clouds. They are sometimes called "mares' tails." They may look like a horse's tail when it is flying in the wind. Cirrus clouds can also look like fish scales. Cirrus clouds often mean that a change in the weather is coming.

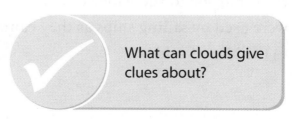

What can clouds give clues about?

Wind

Though we cannot see the wind, we can see what it does. A gentle breeze causes tree branches to sway back and forth. A strong wind bends trees and breaks branches. Wind is another part of weather.

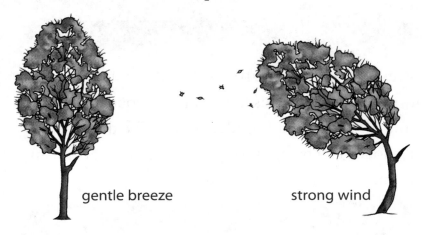

gentle breeze   strong wind

Wind is moving air. Changes in temperature cause air to move. The sun makes the earth warm. This causes air closer to the surface to be warmer than air that is higher. Warmer air rises. Cooler air sinks. As warmer air rises, cooler air moves toward the earth to replace it. This movement of air causes wind.

Some large wind patterns cause wind to blow all the time in certain directions. One large wind pattern causes the trade winds. These winds always blow from Europe to the Americas. They were used by sailing ships as they came to the New World.

trade winds

One of the oldest weather tools is a weather vane. A **weather vane** is a tool that shows which direction the wind is blowing. It is also called a wind vane. The arrow on the weather vane points to the direction the wind is coming from. Most weather vanes have letters that stand for the directions: *N* for north, *S* for south, *E* for east, and *W* for west. When wind blows from the north, the weather vane points to the *N*.

weather vane

The direction of the wind might help us know something about the wind. Winds from the north are usually cold. Winds from the south are usually warm.

We might also want to know how hard the wind is blowing. This is a wind's speed. An **anemometer** is a weather tool that measures wind speed.

anemometer

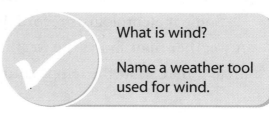

What is wind?

Name a weather tool used for wind.

Studying the Weather

Checking the weather when you wake up helps you know what to wear that day. But to plan future activities you may want to know the weather ahead of time. You may need to know what the weather will be like tomorrow or next week.

Weather Forecasts

Only God knows the future, but scientists can make predictions about what might happen. They study past events to find patterns. They use those patterns to make predictions.

A **meteorologist** is a person who studies the weather. He uses weather tools to collect and record weather data each day. He compares the current data with past weather patterns. This helps him predict what kind of weather is probably coming. A prediction of future weather is called a **weather forecast**.

Meteorologists get some of their data from weather satellites. Weather satellites are sent into space high above the earth. From there they take pictures of the surface of the earth. These pictures show where clouds are. Knowing where clouds are can help meteorologists predict how the weather will change.

Some meteorologists record data on weather maps. A **weather map** shows the weather data over a large area. It may show the temperatures for cities and towns

A meteorologist uses a weather map to show weather data.

close to your area or for cities all across the country. Often it uses colors to show the temperatures of large areas.

A weather map can also show where there is precipitation. It shows whether the precipitation is rain or a form of ice. The precipitation may be shown with symbols or with colors.

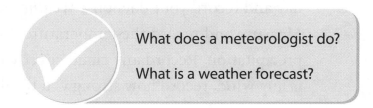

What does a meteorologist do?

What is a weather forecast?

ACTIVITY

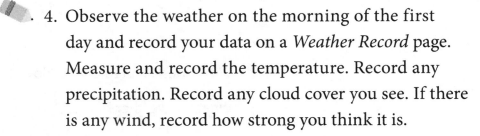

Process skills
- Observing
- Inferring
- Recording data
- Defining operationally

Weather Watcher

Meteorologists use many tools to study and predict the weather. You may not have the same tools that a meteorologist has, but you can use some simple tools to study the weather on your own.

In this activity you will observe and record weather over a period of time. Then you can use your data to make some predictions.

Materials
Weather Record pages
card stock
glue
hole punch
metal brad
thermometer
Activity Manual

Purpose

Observe and record the weather.

Procedure

1. Glue the cloud cards from your Activity Manual onto a piece of card stock.

2. Cut out the cards. Punch a hole in each card at the dot.

3. Attach the cards with the metal brad. You will use this as you observe the clouds.

4. Observe the weather on the morning of the first day and record your data on a *Weather Record* page. Measure and record the temperature. Record any precipitation. Record any cloud cover you see. If there is any wind, record how strong you think it is.

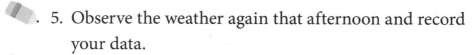
5. Observe the weather again that afternoon and record your data.

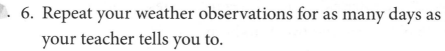
6. Repeat your weather observations for as many days as your teacher tells you to.

Conclusions

▶ Was it sunny or cloudy more often?

▶ Did any cloud type seem to occur most often before a change of weather? If so, which one?

Follow-up

▶ Use other weather tools to collect additional data.

Severe Weather

Sometimes a meteorologist predicts severe weather. Severe weather includes strong thunderstorms, tornadoes, hurricanes, and blizzards. These kinds of weather can cause damage to homes and land.

Strong **thunderstorms** are the kind of severe weather we have most often. A strong thunderstorm has a lot of lightning. The lightning causes the thunder that gives the storm its name. A strong thunderstorm also has heavy rain and strong winds. Sometimes the storm produces hail.

lightning

A thunderstorm can produce another kind of severe weather called a tornado. A **tornado** is a funnel-shaped cloud of swirling winds that reaches the ground. Usually a tornado is only a few hundred meters wide, but its winds are strong. They cause great damage to things that they hit.

tornado

Another kind of severe weather is a hurricane. A **hurricane** has strong, swirling winds and produces heavy rain. A hurricane can be hundreds of kilometers

hurricane

wide. It covers a much larger area than a tornado does. Hurricanes form over warm ocean waters. They mostly affect places near the ocean.

Blizzards are snowstorms with strong winds. In a blizzard the snow blows very hard. It can be hard to see in the blowing snow, and it is easy to get lost. The blowing snow and freezing temperatures make it unsafe to be outside.

blizzard

During severe weather it is best to be inside. In areas where tornados, hurricanes, or blizzards occur, you need to know how to be safe. Talk with your family about what to do if severe weather occurs. You can also prepare an emergency kit. Include supplies such as bottled water, blankets, canned food, flashlights, a radio that uses batteries, and extra batteries.

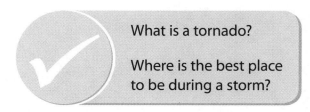

What is a tornado?

Where is the best place to be during a storm?

Words to Know

weather

atmosphere

precipitation

rain gauge

wind

weather vane

anemometer

meteorologist

weather forecast

weather map

thunderstorm

tornado

hurricane

blizzard

Key Ideas

▶ All weather takes place in the atmosphere.

▶ Rain, snow, sleet, and hail are all forms of precipitation.

▶ Evaporation, condensation, and precipitation are parts of the water cycle.

▶ Different kinds of clouds give us clues about the weather.

▶ Wind is caused by changes in temperature.

▶ Lightning and thunder are part of strong thunderstorms.

▶ Hurricanes form over warm ocean water and affect places near the ocean.

▶ During severe weather it is best to be inside.

Write About It

One day you observe the cumulus clouds in the sky getting taller and darker. The wind is also getting stronger. Explain what kind of weather may be on the way and what you should do to be safe.

CHAPTER 10

Psalm 19:1 says, "The heavens declare the glory of God; and the firmament sheweth his handywork." This verse is part of a song written by King David. He wrote many songs to give glory to God. When he was a young shepherd boy, he spent nights outside caring for his sheep. He probably studied the stars and other objects in the night sky. He may have tried to count the stars and noticed how they move throughout the year. The night sky tells about God's glory. Though the stars do not talk, they show us how great God is.

 The Solar System

Look up at the sky on a clear night and you will see thousands of stars. The Bible tells us that "in the beginning God created the heaven and the earth" (Genesis 1:1). We live on the earth. All around us is the earth's atmosphere. Past the atmosphere is the rest of the universe. The earth is just a tiny piece in the huge universe that God created. We can see parts of the rest of the universe when we look at the sky.

God made objects in the sky to have patterns of motion. Each day the sun appears to rise in the east. It appears to move across the sky and set in the west. The pattern happens because the earth rotates. It spins completely around one time each day. The earth's rotation causes us to have day and night.

The earth also moves around the sun. The path around the sun is called an **orbit**. One complete trip around the sun is a year.

The Sun

To us, the sun appears to be the biggest object in the sky. It is very important to the earth. It gives light during the day. It is the major source of energy for the earth. Plants use the sun's energy to make food. We use it to make heat and electricity. The sun heats the air, making it move. The moving air affects our weather.

When we see the sun it does not look like the tiny stars that we see at night. But the sun is a star. It looks big to us because it is much closer to the earth than any other star is. Compared with other stars, it is a medium-sized star. The sun, like other stars, is a ball of burning gas. It gives the light, heat, and energy that are necessary for life on the earth.

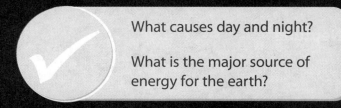

What causes day and night?

What is the major source of energy for the earth?

The Solar System

Earth is a planet. A **planet** is a ball of rock or gas that orbits a star. Earth orbits the sun, but it is not the only planet that orbits the sun. The sun has a total of eight planets that orbit it. These planets are Mercury, Venus, Earth, Mars, Jupiter, Saturn, Uranus, and Neptune. All the planets move around the sun in the same direction but in different orbits.

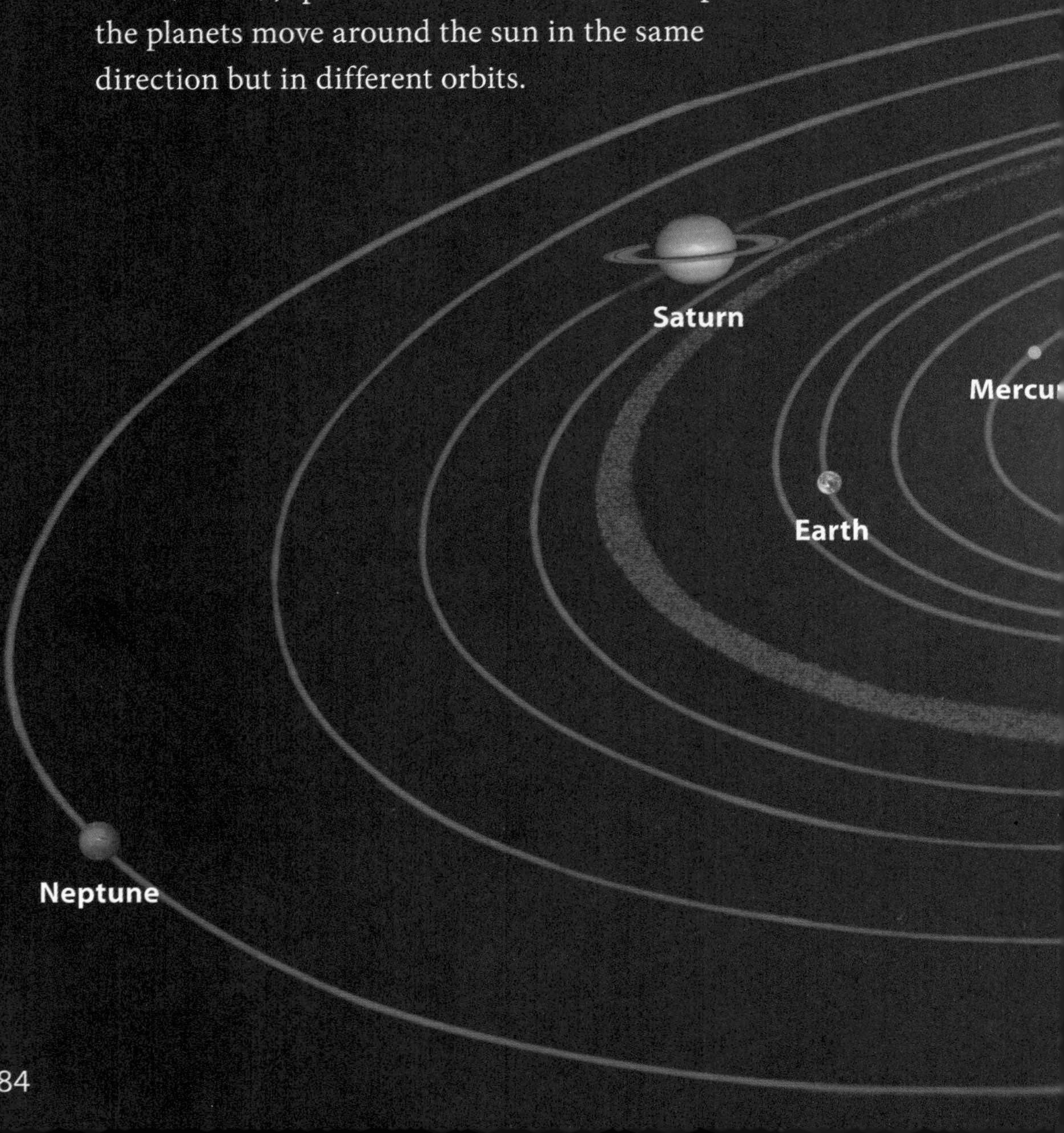

Saturn

Mercu

Earth

Neptune

The sun and the objects that orbit it are called the solar system. The sun is the center of our solar system. It is also the largest object in our solar system. It has most of the mass of the entire solar system.

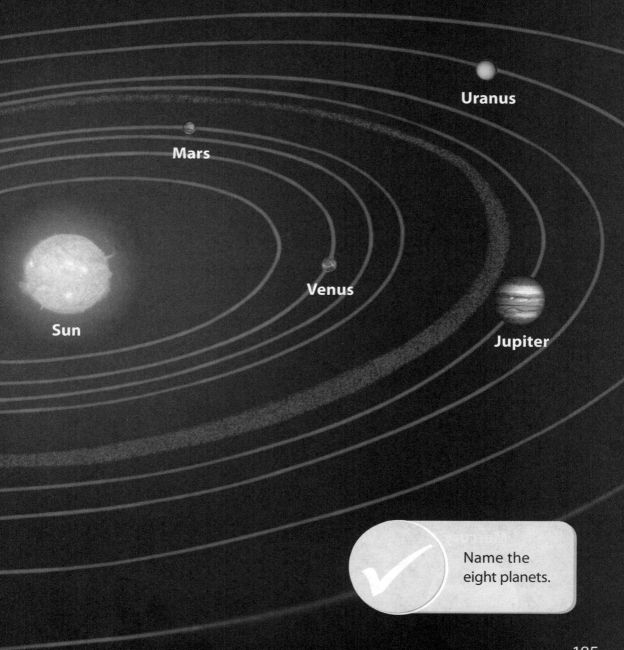

Uranus

Mars

Venus

Jupiter

Sun

✓ Name the eight planets.

Inner Planets

The four planets that are closest to the sun are called rocky planets. These planets are more like Earth than the outer planets are. But Earth is the only planet that has life on it.

Mercury: Closest to the sun

Mercury is the smallest planet and the one closest to the sun. It is only a little larger than our moon. Sometimes Mercury can be seen just after sunset. It is a bright object in the sky, but it is so close to the sun that it is often hard to see.

Mercury has a fast orbit. Its orbit takes less time than any other planet's does. Mercury is closest to the sun, so its path around the sun is the shortest.

Though Mercury orbits quickly, it rotates slowly. This causes it to have huge temperature changes. When facing the sun, it is very hot. When not facing the sun, it gets very cold. The temperature on the side away from the sun falls way below freezing.

Mercury

Mercury   **Venus**

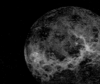

Venus: Earth's twin

Venus is the second planet from the sun. Venus is covered in clouds, and the cloud cover keeps it very hot. It is the hottest planet in our solar system.

Venus is sometimes called Earth's twin. It is just a little smaller than Earth, and its surface is somewhat like Earth's. Scientists have sent spacecraft to the surface of Venus. These space probes have sent back pictures. The pictures show that Venus has plains, volcanoes, mountains, and valleys. But Venus has no water. The clouds are not made of water but of drops of acid.

The clouds around Venus reflect the sun's light. This makes Venus look like a very bright star in the sky. People sometimes call it the morning star or evening star. It is best seen just before sunrise and just after sunset.

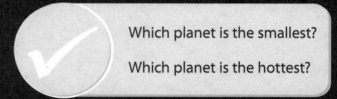

Venus

Which planet is the smallest?

Which planet is the hottest?

Earth: Our home

Earth is the third planet from the sun. It is the only planet with liquid water and an atmosphere that allows life. God perfectly designed Earth for us to live on.

Earth is 150,000,000 kilometers (93,000,000 mi) from the sun. God placed Earth at exactly the right place. If it were closer to the sun, it would be too hot for us to live on. If it were farther away, it would be too cold.

Earth rotates once every 24 hours. This makes one day. The rotation helps keep the temperature from being very hot or very cold. Earth orbits the sun every 365¼ days, which makes one year.

Earth has one moon. The moon takes about 29 days to orbit Earth.

Earth

Moon

Earth

Mars

Mars: The red planet

Mars is the fourth planet from the sun. It is about half the size of Earth. Mars is one of the brightest objects in the night sky. It has a reddish color and is known as the red planet. The whole planet is covered with red dust.

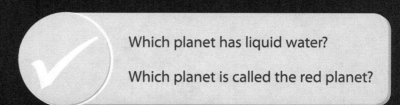

Mars

No one has been to Mars, but scientists still know much about it. It is the most explored planet other than Earth. Space probes have landed on Mars and sent back pictures and information. Space rovers that traveled on Mars's surface have also collected data.

Mars has two moons, named Phobos and Deimos. It also has the highest mountain of any planet in our solar system. This mountain is called Olympus Mons.

Which planet has liquid water?

Which planet is called the red planet?

Outer Planets

The four outer planets have surfaces that are made of gas. These planets are called gas giants because they are so large. They are also far apart. The distance between two of the gas giants is greater than the distance from the sun to Mars.

Jupiter: The largest planet

Jupiter is the fifth planet from the sun. It is the largest planet in our solar system. If Earth were the size of a pea, Jupiter would be the size of a baseball.

Jupiter spins faster than any other planet. Earth rotates every 24 hours. Jupiter takes only about 10 hours to rotate.

Jupiter

Jupiter is covered with colorful clouds of gas. It has a red spot that scientists believe is a huge storm.

Jupiter has at least 63 moons. The four largest are Io, Europa, Ganymede, and Callisto. Each of these moons is bigger than the planet Mercury.

Io   Europa   Ganymede   Callisto

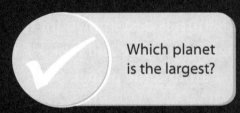

Which planet is the largest?

Jupiter

Saturn: The ringed planet

Saturn is the second-largest planet. It is almost as large as Jupiter. It is also almost twice as far from the sun as Jupiter is.

Saturn is best known for its rings. It has thousands of rings made of ice and rocks. Each ring travels in its own orbit around the planet. Some pieces of the rings are as small as dust, but others are as big as buildings!

Saturn has almost as many moons as Jupiter does. At least 60 of them have been named. The largest one is called Titan. In old Greek stories the Titans were giants. The moon Titan is a giant as well. It is larger than Mars and Mercury combined, and it has its own atmosphere.

Titan

Saturn

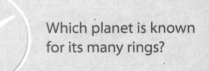

Which planet is known for its many rings?

Saturn

Uranus: The sideways planet

Uranus is pale bluish green. Its color comes from the gases that are around the planet.

Uranus spins in a way no other planet does. Other planets spin tilted slightly away from the sun. The sun shines mostly on their equators. Uranus spins like a top on its side. The sun shines on its poles.

Uranus has at least 11 rings and 27 moons.

Uranus

Neptune: Farthest from the sun

Neptune is known as a blue planet. It is the farthest planet from the sun. Neptune is a very cold planet covered with gas. The wind on the surface of Neptune sometimes blows over 1,600 kilometers (994 mi) per hour.

Triton is Neptune's largest moon. It is one of the coldest objects in space. Neptune also has 12 other moons and several faint rings.

Neptune

Asteroids and Dwarf Planets

Asteroids are small rocky objects in space that orbit the sun. They are many different shapes and sizes. Some are hundreds of miles across. Others are the size of a room in a house. There are also tiny ones that are the size of pebbles. Most asteroids are found in an area between Mars and Jupiter. This area is called an asteroid belt.

asteroid

Dwarf planets are the size of a large asteroid but are round like a ball. Ceres is the largest object in the asteroid belt between Mars and Jupiter. Because of its size and shape, it is called a dwarf planet.

Pluto and Eris are also dwarf planets. Pluto was once called a planet, but it was classified as a dwarf planet in 2006. Eris is the largest dwarf planet. It is also the farthest object scientists have seen to orbit the sun.

Pluto

Which planet is tipped sideways?

Which planet is the farthest from the sun?

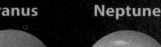
Uranus

Neptune

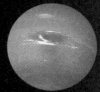

195

ACTIVITY

Solar Mobile

If you were in outer space, you would be amazed at how bright the planets and stars are. Space probes and other space equipment have taken pictures of the planets.

In this activity you will make a mobile that models the order of the planets as they orbit the sun.

Purpose

Make a model of the solar system.

Materials
Planet Bars page
card stock
glue stick
scissors
hole punch
14 pieces of string
Activity Manual

Procedure

1. Glue the *Planet Bars* page onto card stock.

2. Cut out the planet bars by cutting on the dark lines. Be sure to cut the slit marked in the center of each bar.

3. Punch a hole at each dark circle on the planet bars. Place the slits of each bar together so that the bars make an X.

4. Tie one string to each of the four holes at the top near the center of the X. Tie the other ends of those four strings together to make a loop. This loop will allow you to hang your mobile.

5. Paste the sun and planet pictures onto card stock. Cut out the pictures. Punch a hole at the top of each picture.

6. Label each planet by writing its name on the back of its picture. For each planet, choose an interesting fact that you learned about that planet. Write the fact on the back of the picture.

7. Tie a string to each hole marked *S* on the planet bars. Put the ends of both strings through the hole on the sun picture. Tie the strings to the sun.

8. Tie a string to each planet. Arrange the planets in the order they orbit the sun. Tie the first planet to hole 1 of the planet bars. Tie the other planets to their correct places.

Conclusions

▶ What does your mobile model?

▶ Does the mobile correctly model how far apart the planets are?

Follow-up

▶ Make a model that shows how the planets compare in size.

Stars

At night you can usually see many dots of light in the sky. A few of the planets sometimes appear as tiny dots of light. But almost all the dots of light you see are stars.

Stars appear to form **constellations,** or patterns in the sky. The star patterns are similar to dot-to-dot pictures. You may have seen the Big and Little Dippers. These are parts of larger constellations you may be able to see on clear nights.

People have been studying the stars since Bible times. Those who study the stars and planets are called **astronomers.** For a long time people thought that on clear nights they could see all the stars in the universe. Then a man named Galileo used a telescope and saw stars no one had seen before. People found that there are many more things in space than they had thought.

Orion

Big Dipper

Little Dipper

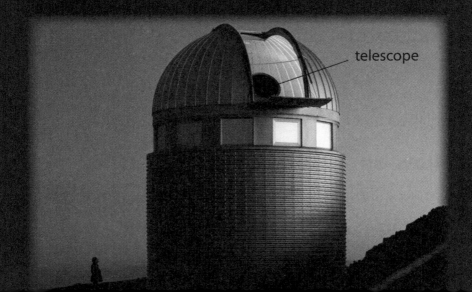

telescope

A **telescope** is a tool that helps us see objects that are far away. We can use it to study objects in space. A telescope is made of curved pieces of glass and mirrors. Astronomers use telescopes to learn many things about the planets and stars. Computers record data from telescopes. The data helps astronomers learn about the universe.

Whether we see the objects in space with a telescope or with just our eyes, we are amazed at the huge universe God created. The greatness of the universe shows the greatness of God.

What do we call a pattern of stars?

What does an astronomer do?

Meet the Scientist
Lyman Spitzer Jr.

In 1946 Lyman Spitzer Jr. suggested putting a telescope in space. He thought a telescope above the earth's atmosphere would get better images. In 1990 the Hubble Space Telescope was launched into space. Spitzer had worked on it for more than 15 years. He stayed active in astronomy until his death in 1997. In 2003 a new space telescope was launched. It is called the Spitzer Space Telescope in his honor.

Words to Know

orbit   astronomer
planet   telescope
constellation

Key Ideas

▶ Objects in the sky have patterns of motion.

▶ The earth's rotation causes day and night.

▶ The sun is a medium-sized star. It is the center of the solar system and the major source of energy on the earth.

▶ The planets in order from the sun outward are Mercury, Venus, Earth, Mars, Jupiter, Saturn, Uranus, and Neptune.

▶ Each of the planets has certain characteristics that help identify it.

▶ God perfectly designed the earth for us to live on.

▶ There is a belt of asteroids between Mars and Jupiter.

▶ Pluto is a dwarf planet.

Write About It

The sun is actually a star. Write a few sentences telling why the sun seems different to us from other stars and how important the sun is to the earth.

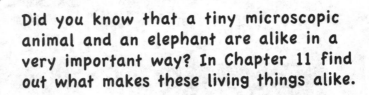

Did you know that a tiny microscopic animal and an elephant are alike in a very important way? In Chapter 11 find out what makes these living things alike.

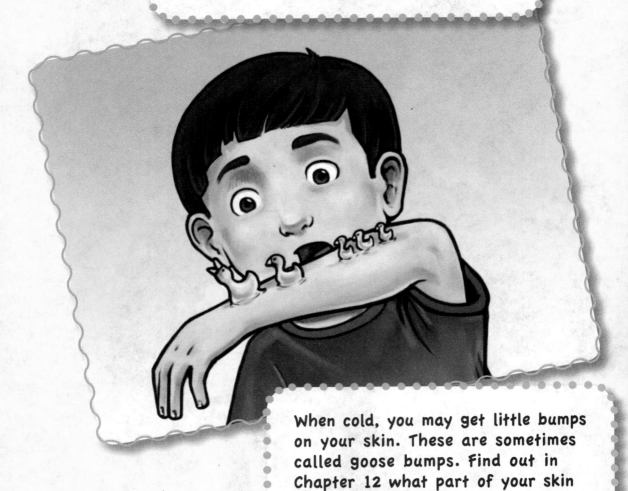

When cold, you may get little bumps on your skin. These are sometimes called goose bumps. Find out in Chapter 12 what part of your skin causes these bumps to occur.

CHAPTER 11

God knows about every small cell in us even before we are born. The Bible tells us about a special baby God knew about. An angel appeared to a priest named Zachariah. The angel said Zachariah's wife would have a baby. The baby's name would be John. John would be "great in the sight of the Lord."

Zachariah did not believe at first. His wife was too old to have a baby. Because Zachariah did not believe, he could not talk until the angel's words came true. When the baby was born, Zachariah wrote that the baby's name was John. Then Zachariah was able to speak again, and he praised God.

Cells, Tissues, and Organs

For many years scientists did not know what plants and animals were made of. Then an instrument was invented that allowed scientists to see parts of plants and animals that they could not see before. That instrument was the microscope.

A **microscope** is a tool that magnifies tiny things. It lets us see things that are too small for us to see without help.

About 350 years ago an English scientist named Robert Hooke looked at a piece of cork under a microscope. Cork is a type of plant. He wrote down what the cork looked like up close.

Robert Hooke wrote about "little boxes" in his report. He thought these boxes looked like rooms or chambers. He called these little boxes cells. The word *cell* comes from a Latin word meaning "chamber."

Many scientists began to use microscopes to help them find out about things. When they placed a piece of living material, such as a leaf, under the microscope, they could see tiny structures for the first time. Imagine how exciting that was! Scientists could see things that they never could before.

Scientists began to observe plants and animals under microscopes. Over time scientists learned that all living things are made of cells.

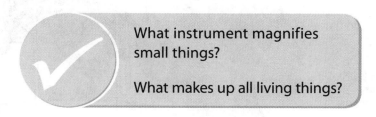

What instrument magnifies small things?

What makes up all living things?

Cells

Kinds of Cells

A **cell** is the smallest living part of any living thing. Most cells can be seen only under a microscope.

Cells come in many shapes. Some, such as the ones seen by Robert Hooke, look like little boxes. Others look like rods, circles, coils, or even blobs of jelly.

Cells also come in many sizes. Some cells are so small that if 50,000 of them were lined up, the row would be only a little more than 2 centimeters long. Some cells are rather large. The yolk of an egg is one cell. The largest single cell is the yolk of an ostrich egg.

Plants and animals are made up of many cells. The size of a living thing is related to the number of cells it has. An elephant has millions of cells. Huge redwood trees also have millions of cells.

Some living things are made of only one cell. You can see them with a microscope. An amoeba is a single-celled creature. It is about half the size of the period at the end of a sentence. It looks like a blob of jelly and lives in water or moist soil.

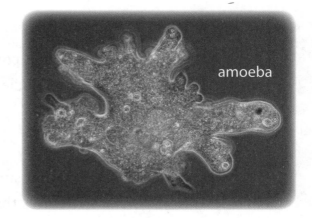

amoeba

Another single-celled creature is a paramecium. It is shaped like a flattened football. A large paramecium can be about the size of a period. You may be able to see it with a magnifying glass.

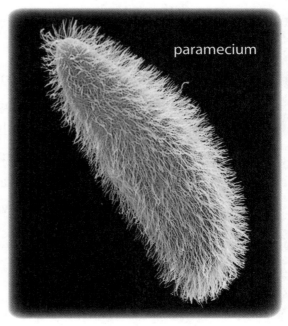

paramecium

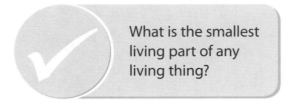

What is the smallest living part of any living thing?

Parts of Cells

Whether big or small, all cells have the same main parts. God designed each part to do a different job for the cell.

Nucleus

The **nucleus** of a cell is its control center. It regulates the activities of the cell. The nucleus looks like a large, dark part in the cell.

Cytoplasm

Cytoplasm is a fluid that surrounds the nucleus. It looks like thin jelly. The structures that help the cell live and grow are in the cytoplasm.

Boundaries

Each cell has a soft, thin covering called a **cell membrane**. This membrane forms a boundary that holds the cytoplasm in place. Plant and animal cells both have cell membranes.

Plant cells also have cell walls. The **cell wall** is a layer on the outside of the cell membrane. The cell wall is stiffer than the cell membrane. The cell wall gives the plant support.

Animal Cell

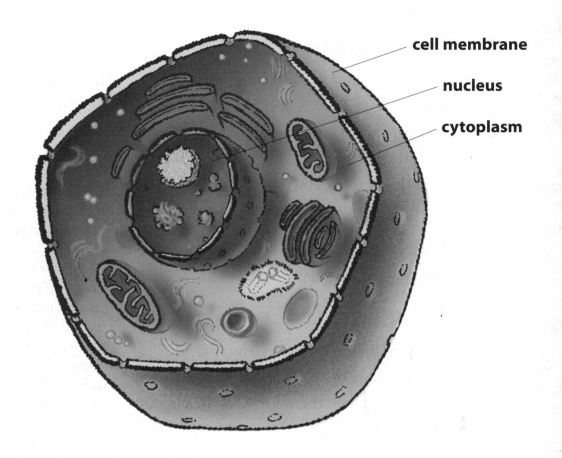

cell membrane

nucleus

cytoplasm

Name the three main parts of a cell.

What boundary does a plant cell have in addition to the cell membrane?

ACTIVITY

Edible Cell

When things are too small for us to see without an instrument to help us, it is helpful to have a model. To see a cell we need a microscope, but using a model helps us learn about the parts.

In this activity you will make a model of an animal cell. Then you can eat your "cell"!

Purpose

Model an animal cell.

Procedure

1. Place the rolled fruit strip around the inside of the cup. The fruit strip should touch the bottom of the cup all the way around.

2. Mix the hot water and gelatin powder in a bowl. Stir until the powder is dissolved.

3. Add ½ cup of ice cubes to the gelatin mixture. Stir until the ice melts.

4. Pour gelatin into the cup until it reaches the top of the fruit strip.

5. Fill the other bowl with ice. Place the gelatin cup in the bowl of ice. Cover the bowl with a towel.

Materials
clear plastic cup, 9 oz
rolled fruit strip
measuring cups
1 cup hot water
gelatin powder
spoon
2 bowls
ice cubes
towel
round gumball

6. Let the gelatin sit until it is firm and not a liquid. Take the cup out of the ice bowl. Push the gumball into the gelatin.

7. Display your model and then eat your "cell."

Conclusions

▶ What part of your model represents cytoplasm?

▶ What part of a cell does the rolled fruit strip represent?

Follow-up

▶ Add another food item to change your model of an animal cell into a plant cell model.

Tissues

A cell does all the things that a living thing does. It needs food. It grows. It uses energy. It reproduces.

Sometimes a cell works alone. Single-celled creatures are examples of this. In most living things, though, groups of cells work together. A **tissue** is a group of cells all doing the same kind of work.

There are two kinds of tissues that a plant uses to make and move food—xylem and phloem. Xylem moves water from the roots to the leaves for photosynthesis. After the plant makes food, phloem moves the food to other parts of the plant.

God gave people special kinds of tissues too. Epithelial, connective, muscle, and nerve tissues are the four main kinds of tissues in the human body. Each has an important job.

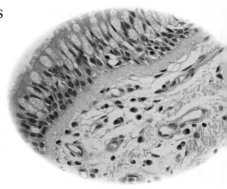

Epithelial tissue is smooth tissue. Its job is to provide covering and protection. The outside of your skin is this kind of tissue. Epithelial tissue also lines the insides of your mouth, throat, and parts of your lungs.

epithelial tissue

Connective tissue holds parts of your body together. Bones and fat are connective tissues. Blood is also a special kind of connective tissue. Your body has more connective tissue than any other kind.

connective tissue

Muscle tissue allows your body to move. You can see and feel some of your muscles as they work. Other muscles, such as the ones that help you digest your food or cause your heart to beat, you cannot see. All your muscles, though, are very important.

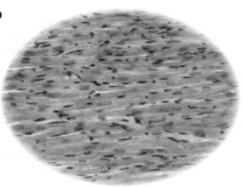

muscle tissue

Nerve tissue carries messages between your body and your brain. The messages tell your body what is happening and what to do. They allow you to respond to the things around you. Nerve tissue has billions of tiny connecting fibers. These fibers "talk" to each other by passing signals back and forth.

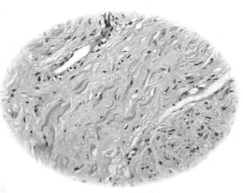

nerve tissue

What name do we give a group of cells all doing the same kind of work?

Name four kinds of tissues in your body.

Organs

A group of tissues working together is an **organ**. Organs are the major parts of the body. An organ may use several different kinds of tissue. A good example is the eye. This organ uses muscle tissue to focus. The nerve tissue sends a message to the brain to tell what is seen. Each tissue in the eye has its own job, but the tissues also work together. When all the tissues do their jobs, the eye can do its job.

God gave your organs important jobs. Your eyes let you see. Your lungs allow you to breathe. Your heart pumps blood to your body. Your stomach helps you digest food. Your brain is the control center for your body. These are just a few of the many organs in your body.

brain

heart

lungs

stomach

Systems

A group of organs working together makes a **system**. One system in your body is the digestive system. The stomach is part of this system, but other organs are as well. The tongue, esophagus, liver, and small and large intestines all work together to digest your food.

Cells make up tissues. Tissues form organs. Organs work together to form systems.

cell ➔ tissue ➔ organ ➔ system

Each part of the body has its own job. But different parts of the body also help each other. For the body to work right, all the parts must work together. The Bible reminds us that Christians should also work together. First Corinthians 12:25 says that "the members should have the same care one for another." Christians can care for each other by faithfully doing their own jobs and by working together to get jobs done.

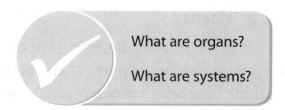

What are organs?

What are systems?

Diving Deep into Science

Words to Know

microscope	cytoplasm	tissue
cell	cell membrane	organ
nucleus	cell wall	system

Key Ideas

▶ Robert Hooke gave the boxes he saw the name *cells*.

▶ All living things are made of cells.

▶ Cells come in many shapes and sizes.

▶ An amoeba is a single-celled creature.

▶ All cells have the same main parts.

▶ In the human body there are four main kinds of tissues.

▶ Epithelial tissue, such as skin, provides covering and protection.

▶ Connective tissue, such as bones and fat, holds the body together.

▶ Muscle tissue allows the body to move.

▶ Nerve tissue carries messages between the body and the brain.

▶ An organ may have more than one kind of tissue.

▶ The lungs, heart, stomach, and brain are organs.

Write About It

A cell is the smallest living part of the body. Tissues, organs, and systems are larger parts of the body. Write a paragraph explaining how cells, tissues, organs, and systems are related to each another.

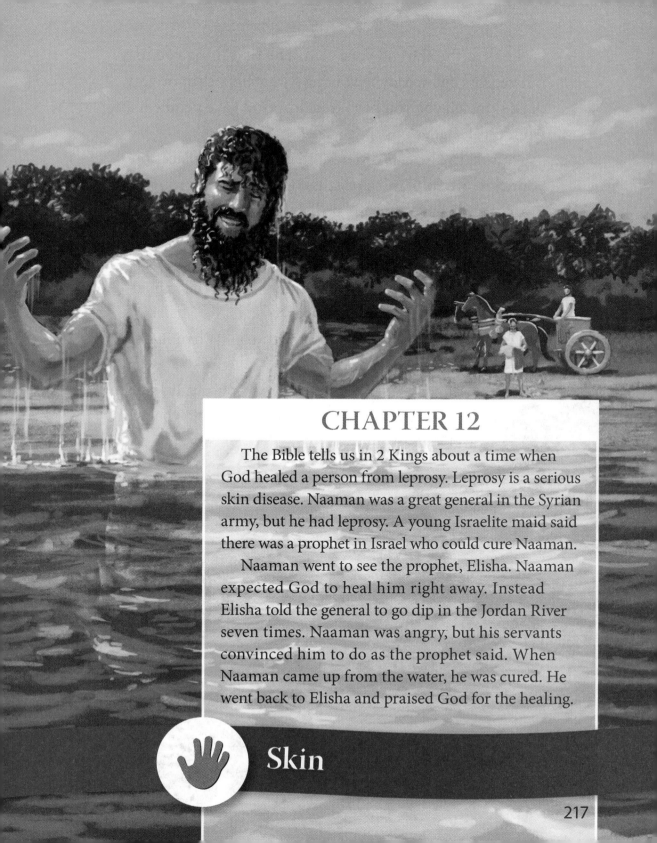

CHAPTER 12

The Bible tells us in 2 Kings about a time when God healed a person from leprosy. Leprosy is a serious skin disease. Naaman was a great general in the Syrian army, but he had leprosy. A young Israelite maid said there was a prophet in Israel who could cure Naaman.

Naaman went to see the prophet, Elisha. Naaman expected God to heal him right away. Instead Elisha told the general to go dip in the Jordan River seven times. Naaman was angry, but his servants convinced him to do as the prophet said. When Naaman came up from the water, he was cured. He went back to Elisha and praised God for the healing.

Skin

Look at the skin on your arm. The first thing you may notice is its color. Maybe you have very light skin or very dark skin. Maybe you have freckles. God gave people many wonderful shades of skin.

Your skin also has different textures. Some places on your skin are thin and smooth. Other places are rough. Your eyelids have smooth skin. The skin on the bottoms of your feet is usually rough.

Skin folds and stretches. Your elbows and knees bend many times during a day. Each time they do, the skin at those places stretches and goes back.

As you grow, your skin grows with you. When it gets hurt or torn, it can even heal itself!

God made your skin to cover your body. It protects your muscles, bones, and organs. Imagine what you would look like without it!

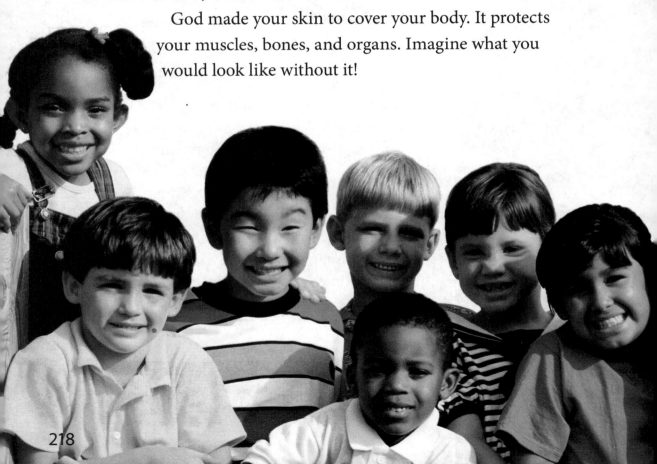

Layers of Skin

Every organ in your body has a function, or job, to do. An organ is made of many cells and tissues working together. Your skin is the largest organ in your body. Though it has many parts, it has just two layers. The **epidermis** is the top layer of the skin. Under the epidermis is the second layer, which is called the **dermis**.

Even though you cannot see anything happening, your skin is hard at work. New skin cells are always being made in the lowest part of the epidermis. As the new cells move to the surface, they push older cells ahead of them. After a while the old, dead skin cells at the surface of the epidermis fall off.

The epidermis is always losing old skin cells. You do many things that help remove dead cells. Washing your skin or even just changing your clothes removes some dead cells.

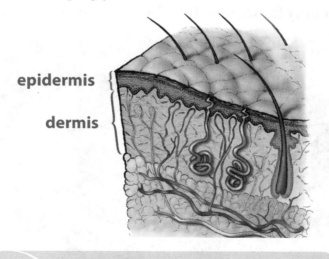

epidermis

dermis

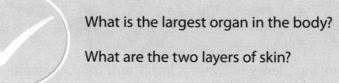

What is the largest organ in the body?

What are the two layers of skin?

The Epidermis

God made skin to be a marvelous protection for your body. Although the epidermis is very thin, it works like a strong shield. It helps keep harmful things out of your body. Dirt and germs cannot pass through the skin. If these things could get through, you would get sick much more often.

The epidermis also keeps in things that your body needs. One important thing your body needs is water. Water keeps your body from drying out. It helps keep your body's organs working properly and keeps your blood flowing.

Water also helps keep your body at the right temperature. When you get warm, water comes out on your skin to help you cool down. It is important to drink plenty of water. Your body needs to replace the water you lose. A cold drink of water not only tastes good but also helps keep you healthy.

Drinking plenty of water is important for your health.

The sun causes your skin to make more melanin.

The epidermis has a substance called melanin. **Melanin** is the coloring in your skin. The more melanin you have, the darker your skin. When you are in the sun more, the cells in your epidermis make more melanin. Your skin gets darker.

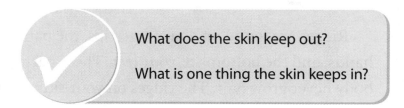

What does the skin keep out?

What is one thing the skin keeps in?

Fingerprints

The epidermis has many lines and grooves in it. If you look closely at your fingertips, you can see dozens of curved ridges. The prints made by the ridges on your fingertips are called **fingerprints**. Each person in the world has his own set of fingerprints. Even identical twins have different prints.

Fingerprints help to identify people. When you were born, a nurse made a copy of your footprint or handprint. The print is a record that can identify who you are.

Fingerprints are used in many ways. Policemen use them to help identify criminals. Schools and some businesses use fingerprints to identify who is working for them. In some places fingerprints are used like a key. A machine scans a person's finger. If the print matches the machine's records, the person is allowed to pass through the door. There are even some computers that use a fingerprint as the "password" to use the computer.

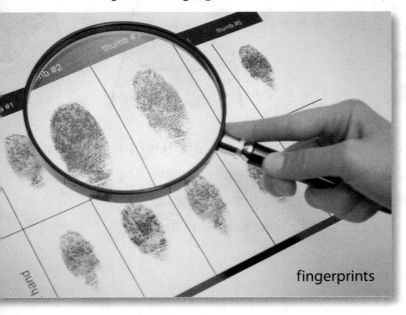

fingerprints

Ridges are found on your fingertips, the palms of your hands, and the bottoms of your feet. These parts of your body never grow hair. The ridges on your skin are formed

The ridges on your fingers help you grip things.

in the deepest layers of the skin. The ridges were formed even before you were born. They will be the same your whole life.

The ridges on your fingers are not there only to identify you. They are also useful for the tasks that you do every day. They help you pick things up. They also help keep objects from slipping out of your grasp. Without the ridges on your skin, it would be hard for you to pick up a glass.

Think of trying to hold on to a glass when your hands are wet. The water on your hands fills in the ridges on your fingers. This makes it harder to grip the glass.

What are fingerprints?

Patterns on My Skin

No one else has the same fingerprints as you. However, there are three main fingerprint patterns. Some fingerprints have arches. Others have loops. Still others have whorls.

In this activity you will record your fingerprints and compare them to the patterns. Which pattern best matches your fingerprints?

Purpose

Identify and compare fingerprint patterns.

Materials
Fingerprint Card page
washable ink pad
damp paper towels
Activity Manual

Procedure

1. Fill out the first two rows of your fingerprint card.

2. Gently roll your right thumb across the ink pad. Roll your thumb at a steady speed. Find the spot on the card for your right thumb. Press down lightly, rolling your thumb again from side to side.

3. Repeat step 2 with each finger on your right hand. Clean your hand.

4. Repeat steps 2–3 with your left hand, doing each finger separately.

5. Put all four fingers of your left hand on the ink pad. Find the square marked *Left Four Fingers*. Keep your fingers straight. Do not bend or roll them. Press your

hand and all four fingers down flat at the same time. Clean your fingers.

6. Repeat step 5 with your right hand. Then ink your thumbs and put your thumbprints between the fingerprint groups. Clean your thumbs. Your card should show each print individually and then the prints as a group.

7. Compare your fingerprints with the patterns in your Activity Manual. Decide which pattern best matches your prints. Then compare your prints with other people's.

Conclusions

▶ Which pattern best matches your fingerprints?

▶ Are your fingerprints similar to anyone else's?

Follow-up

▶ Make a graph showing how many people in your class or family have each fingerprint pattern.

The Dermis

The dermis is much thicker than the epidermis. It has a different job to do for your body. It contains the nerves, blood vessels, sweat glands, and oil glands.

Nerves

Nerves are small but important parts of the dermis. The nerves allow you to feel things. They constantly send messages to your brain. Some nerves tell you how things feel. Some tell you when something hurts. Others tell you whether you are hot or cold.

All of your dermis has nerves. But some areas have more nerves than others. You use your fingers and hands to touch things. God designed the skin on your fingers and hands to have many nerves. Places such as your back and your ear lobes have fewer nerves.

God gave you nerves in your skin to protect you. They help you prevent injury. For example, without nerves you could not feel whether something is hot. Your nerves make you feel pain so you can avoid getting badly burned.

Fantastic Facts

When you get cold you might notice your skin is covered with little bumps. These bumps are called goose bumps or goose pimples, but they have nothing to do with geese. The nerves in your skin cause the hair on your skin to stand erect. This causes bumps. Goose bumps can also appear when you are scared.

What layer of skin contains nerves?

Blood vessels

The blood vessels in your dermis have a very important job. They help keep your body at a constant temperature. They do this by getting wider or narrower. When you get hot, the blood vessels become wider. They allow more blood to come near the skin's surface. This helps your body release some of its heat. When the blood vessels are narrower, most of the blood is kept deeper inside your body. This helps your body keep its heat in.

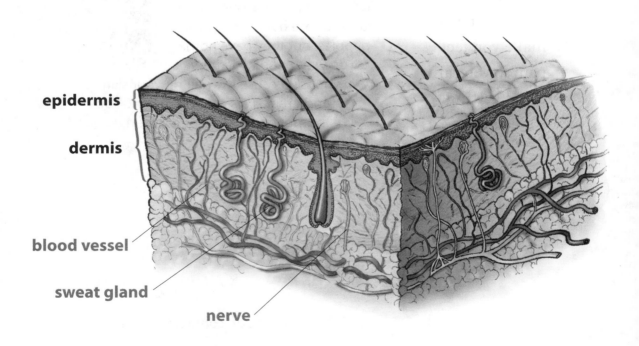

epidermis

dermis

blood vessel

sweat gland

nerve

There are no blood vessels in the epidermis. If you lightly scratch your palm, nothing will happen. If blood vessels were in your epidermis, you would bleed easily.

When you get warm, more blood than usual comes to your skin. This blood is carrying heat from inside your body. When the blood comes close to the surface of your skin, your pores open. **Pores** are tiny openings on the surface of your skin. When the pores open, they allow your body to get rid of extra heat.

Sweat glands

God gave your body another way to cool down as well. Your skin has special structures called **sweat glands** that move water to the skin's surface. There the body releases the water. The drops of water on the surface of the skin are called **perspiration**, or sweat. As the water evaporates, your body cools down.

How do blood vessels help control the body's temperature?

What structures move water to the surface of the skin?

Oil glands

Most of your body has hair. Hair is made up of dead cells. It does not hurt to cut hair, but it does hurt to pull out a strand of hair. Each strand of hair starts in a hair follicle in the dermis. There are nerves around the hair follicle. If you pull out a hair, you feel pain from the surrounding nerves.

Near the base of each hair is an oil gland. **Oil glands** release oil, which helps protect your body. Oil keeps your skin soft and waterproof. It also keeps moisture inside your skin. Without it, the water in your body would come out too quickly and your skin would dry out.

The oil also protects your skin from infection. The oil and hair work together to trap dirt on the skin until it can be washed off. That is why it is important to keep your skin and hair clean.

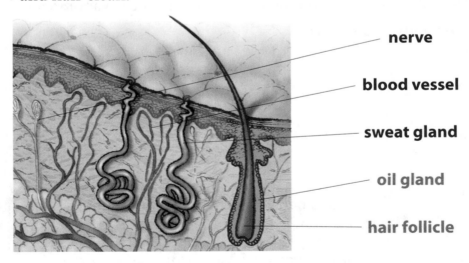

nerve

blood vessel

sweat gland

oil gland

hair follicle

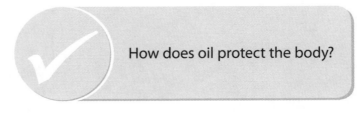

How does oil protect the body?

You can see only the epidermis layer of your skin. But most of the important parts of your skin are in the dermis. In this exploration you will make a model that shows all the parts of the skin.

What to Do

1. Get a stiff piece of cardboard or poster board. With a pencil, sketch a large diagram of the skin. Use the diagrams on pages 228 and 230 as examples.

2. Use two colors of modeling clay, one for each layer of skin. Press the clay down firmly so it sticks to the board.

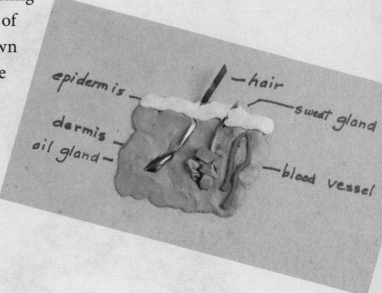

3. Use plastic lacing or colored yarn to show blood vessels, sweat glands, oil glands, and hair.

4. Label the parts of your model.

Skin Care

Keeping clean is the easiest way to help your skin. It is also the best way to keep from getting sick. Germs, dirt, and oil can get trapped on the skin. Use soap, water, and a clean washcloth to remove dirt and dead cells.

Your hair and nails also trap dirt. Washing your hair and fingernails helps remove the dirt and extra oil. Your nails should be cut or filed. They should not be bitten. Biting your nails puts the dirt trapped under them into your mouth.

Sunlight is good for you, but too much sun can burn your skin. You should be careful to protect your skin from too much sun. Clothing covers some of your skin. Sunscreen can protect your exposed skin.

Sunscreen helps protect your skin from getting burned by the sun.

You can also protect your skin by being careful around sharp objects. Cuts in your skin require special care. They can allow harmful things to enter your body. Dirt and germs can be trapped deep in the skin.

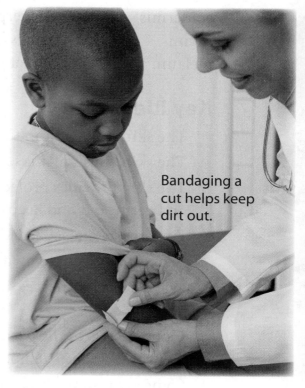

Bandaging a cut helps keep dirt out.

If you get a cut, clean it with soap and water to remove any dirt. You may need to put medicine on it. It is also a good idea to cover a cut with a bandage. Covering the cut helps keep dirt out.

Cuts should be checked by an adult. Some cuts may require a visit to a doctor. Proper care of a cut helps it heal quickly.

We often do not think about our skin unless it gets hurt. But it is always working to keep us safe and healthy. God, the Creator, designed each part of the body just right. In Psalm 139:14 the Bible says, "I will praise thee; for I am fearfully and wonderfully made."

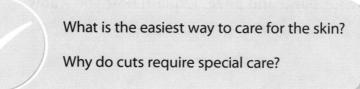

What is the easiest way to care for the skin?

Why do cuts require special care?

Words to Know

epidermis	fingerprint	perspiration
dermis	pores	oil gland
melanin	sweat gland	

Key Ideas

▶ The skin is an organ. It has two layers.

▶ The skin constantly loses dead cells of the epidermis.

▶ The skin provides protection for the body. It keeps dirt and germs out and keeps water in.

▶ Fingers have raised ridges on them.

▶ Each person has his own set of fingerprints.

▶ The dermis has nerves, blood vessels, sweat glands, and oil glands.

▶ Blood vessels in the dermis widen and narrow to help control the body's temperature.

▶ Some areas of the body have more nerves than other areas do.

▶ Cuts in the skin require special care.

Write About It

You fall on a sidewalk and scrape your palm and your knee. Your palm does not bleed, but your knee does. Write a paragraph telling which layer or layers of skin were injured on your hand and knee. Explain how you know.

Glossary

A

amphibian A cold-blooded animal that lives part of its life in water and part on land.

anemometer A tool that measures the speed of wind.

astronomer A person who studies the stars and planets.

atmosphere The blanket of air that surrounds the earth.

B

balance A tool used to compare a known amount of matter with an unknown amount.

bedrock The layer of large, unbroken rock underneath the subsoil.

bird A warm-blooded animal that has feathers.

blizzard A snowstorm with strong winds.

C

camouflage The blending in of something with its surroundings.

carnivore A consumer that eats other consumers instead of eating plants.

cell The smallest living part of a living thing.

cell membrane A soft, thin covering that forms the boundary of a cell.

cell wall The firm outside boundary of a plant cell.

chemical change A change in matter that forms a new substance.

chlorophyll The green coloring found in a plant's chloroplasts.

chloroplasts The tiny parts of a plant's leaf that help the plant make food.

cold-blooded A term describing an animal whose body temperature changes depending on its surroundings.

community All the different living things in an ecosystem.

condensation The process by which gas changes to a liquid.

constellation A group of stars that forms a pattern or picture in the sky.

consumer An organism that depends on producers for food. A consumer cannot get energy directly from the sun.

cytoplasm A jellylike fluid that surrounds the nucleus of a cell.

D

decomposer An organism that helps break down dead things and wastes.

dermis The layer of skin under the epidermis.

drought A condition that occurs when an area does not receive enough precipitation.

E

echo A sound that reflects clearly and is heard again.

ecosystem All the living things and their environment within a certain area.

energy The ability to do work.

environment The nonliving things that surround a living thing.

epidermis The top layer of skin.

evaporation The process by which a liquid changes to a gas.

F

fingerprints The prints made by the curved ridges on fingertips.

fish A cold-blooded animal that lives in water.

food chain The transfer of energy through an ecosystem.

food web Several food chains linked together.

force A push or a pull.

fossil Any part or mark of a living thing that is naturally preserved after it dies.

friction A force that slows or stops motion.

G

gas The state of matter that has no definite volume or shape.

graduated container A container used for measurement that has lines and numbers marked on its sides.

gram (g) The standard metric unit of measurement for mass.

gravity A force that pulls objects toward the center of the earth.

H

habitat The place where a population lives.

herbivore A consumer that eats only plants.

humus The part of topsoil formed from the remains of living things that have died and decayed.

hurricane A storm of strong, swirling winds and heavy rain that forms over the ocean.

I

igneous rock Rock formed when hot, melted rock cools and hardens.

instinct The basic knowledge and skills that an animal is born with.

invertebrate An animal that does not have a backbone.

L

learned behavior A behavior that an animal learns to do.

liquid The state of matter that has a definite volume but no definite shape.

liter (L) The standard metric unit of measurement for volume.

M

mammal A warm-blooded animal that has hair or fur and feeds its young with milk.

marine mammal A mammal that lives in the sea.

marsupial A mammal, such as a kangaroo, that has a pouch.

mass The amount of material that an object has.

matter Anything that has mass and takes up space.

melanin The coloring in the skin.

metamorphic rock Rock formed when an igneous or sedimentary rock is changed by great heat and pressure.

meteorologist A person who studies the weather.

meter (m) The standard metric unit of measurement for length and distance.

microscope A tool that magnifies tiny things.

mineral A solid material in nature that was never alive, such as iron, salt, and gold.

mixture The combination of two or more kinds of matter.

motion A change in position.

N

nucleus The control center of a cell.

O

oil gland A special structure in the skin that releases oil onto the skin.

omnivore A consumer that eats both plants and other consumers.

orbit The path a planet takes around the sun.

organ A group of tissues working together.

P

perspiration The drops of water released onto the skin as sweat.

photosynthesis The process by which plants make food.

physical change A change in matter that does not form a new substance.

physical property A characteristic of matter that can be observed.

pitch The highness or lowness of a sound.

planet A ball of rock or gas that orbits a star.

population All the plants or animals of the same kind that live in an ecosystem.

pore A tiny opening on the surface of the skin that allows heat and water to leave the body.

precipitation The water that falls from the sky to the ground.

predator An animal that hunts and eats other animals.

prey An animal that a predator hunts.

producer An organism, such as a plant, that makes its own food. A producer gets its energy directly from the sun.

Q

quality The characteristic of sound that makes a sound different from all others.

R

rain gauge A tool used to measure rainfall.

reptile A cold-blooded animal that has tough, dry, scaly skin.

rock A hard piece of the earth's surface.

S

sedimentary rock Rock formed when layers of sediment are pressed together and harden.

soil The loose material on the earth's surface.

solid The state of matter that has a definite shape and volume.

sound A vibration you can hear.

stomata The tiny openings on the underside of plant leaves.

stored energy Energy that can be changed into a form of work.

subsoil The second layer of soil, which contains large pieces of rock.

sweat gland A special structure in the skin that moves water up to the surface of the skin.

system A group of organs working together.

T

telescope A tool used to study faraway objects, such as planets and stars.

tissue A group of cells all doing the same kind of work.

topsoil The top layer of soil. Plants grow in this layer.

tornado A funnel-shaped cloud of swirling winds that reaches the ground.

V

vertebrate An animal that has a backbone.

vibration A rapid back-and-forth movement.

volcano An opening in the earth that allows melted rock to come to the surface.

volume 1. The amount of space that an object takes up. 2. The loudness or softness of a sound.

W

warm-blooded A term describing an animal that has about the same body temperature all the time.

weather The condition of the air at a certain time and place.

weather forecast A prediction of future weather conditions.

weathering The breaking down of rocks.

weather vane A tool that shows from which direction the wind is blowing.

weight The amount of force gravity has on an object.

wind Moving air.

work Occurs when a force moves something.

Index

G

gas, 46, 48, 90–91, 96–97
graduated container, 86–87
gram, 85
gravity, 128, 135

H

habitat, 63
herbivore, 66, 68
humus, 147–48
hurricane, 178–79

I

igneous rock, 152–53
instinct, 36–37
invertebrate, 4–5

L

learned behavior, 36–37
liquid, 89, 91, 94–98
liter, 86

M

mammal, 30–35
marsupial, 35
mass, 83–85
Matter, 82–91, 94–98, 100–102
    changes to, 100–102
    states of, 88–91, 94–98

melanin, 221
metamorphic rock, 155
meteorologist, 174–75
meter, 50
microscope, 204–7
mineral, 156–59
mixture, 100
motion, 128, 132–33

N

nucleus, 208–9

O

oil gland, 230
omnivore, 66–67
orbit, 182
organ, 214–15, 219

P

perspiration, 229
photosynthesis, 46–49, 64
physical change, 100–101
physical property, 83
pitch, 118
Planet, 184–94
    Earth, 182–83, 188
    Jupiter, 190–91
    Mars, 189

Photograph Credits

The following agencies and individuals have furnished materials to meet the photographic needs of this textbook. We wish to express our gratitude to them for their important contribution.

AGI Image Bank
Alamy
ArtINeed, Inc.
Avery Weigh-Tronix, LLC
David W. Boyd Jr.
Stephen Christopher
CORBIS
Department of Energy, National Renewable
    Energy Laboratory (DOE/NREL)
Earthscienceworld.org
European Organization for Astronomical
    Research in the Southern Hemisphere
    (ESO)
Fotolia.com
Getty Images
Warren Gretz
Jeff Henry
Ideals Publications
istockphoto.com
JupiterImages Corporation
Breck P. Kent
Media Bakery
Rita Mitchell
NASA
NASA Goddard Space Flight Center (NASA-
    GSFC)
PhotoDisc, Inc.
Photo Researchers, Inc.
Salter Brecknell Weighing Products
Solar and Heliospheric Observatory (SOHO)
Stockxpert.com
United States Geological Survey (USGS)
Unusual Films
Visuals Unlimited
Wikimedia Commons
Wikipedia

Unit 1 Opener
www.istockphoto.com/Vincent Dale 1

Chapter 1
© Gerald and Buff Corsi/Visuals Unlimited 4; www.istockphoto.com/Milos Luzanin 5 (top); www.istockphoto.com/Maria Bibikova 5 (middle); PhotoDisc/Getty Images 5 (bottom), 14 (all); www.istockphoto.com/ Edwin van Wier 8, 9; Breck P. Kent 12 (top); www.istockphoto.com/David Coder 12 (middle); www.istockphoto.com/Dieter Spears 12 (bottom); © Cosmos Blank/Photo Researchers, Inc. 15 (left); Getty Images 15 (right); © E. R. Degginger/Photo Researchers, Inc. 16; © 2008 JupiterImages Corporation 18; Unusual Films 21

Chapter 2
PhotoDisc/Getty Images 25 (top), 26 (top), 30 (top), 32 (top left); www.istockphoto.com/ Kitch Bain 25 (middle); www.istockphoto.com/ James Richey 25 (bottom); www.istockphoto .com/Ai-Lan Lee 26 (bottom); © 2008 JupiterImages Corporation 27 (top), 32 (right), 33 (bottom right), 34 (bottom); © Dirk V. Mallinckrodt/Alamy 27 (bottom); www .istockphoto.com/lightasafeather 28 (top); © Dr. Dan Sudia/Photo Researchers, Inc. 28 (bottom); www.istockphoto.com/Steven Love 30 (middle); www.istockphoto.com/Holger Mette 30 (bottom); © Peter Chadwick/Photo Researchers, Inc. 31; www.istockphoto.com/ Karen Massier 32 (bottom left); Andre © Fotolia 33 (top left); www.istockphoto.com/ Gijs Bekenkamp 33 (bottom left); Stockxpert .com/JupiterImages Corporation 33 (top right); www.istockphoto.com/Richard Schmidt-Zuper 34 (top); www.istockphoto .com/Peggy Easterly 34 (middle); www .istockphoto.com/Sandra Caldwell 35 (top); Design Pics Inc./Alamy 35 (bottom); © Carolyn A. McKeone/Photo Researchers, Inc. 36 (top); © Robert Ryals/Alamy 36 (middle); © Joe McDonald/Visuals Unlimited

36 (bottom); Unusual Films. Photo includes My Book of Wild Animals, © 2007 by the Zoological Society of San Diego, by permission of Ideals Publications 39

Unit 2 Opener
irina2005 © Fotolia 41

Chapter 3
PhotoDisc/Getty Images 44, 55 (all); Breck P. Kent 46; David W. Boyd Jr. 47; Rita Mitchell 50 (all); Unusual Films 53; www.istockphoto .com/Robyn Mackenzie 54 (top); © 2008 JupiterImages Corporation 54 (middle left, middle right, bottom), 56 (all); Courtesy of DOE/NREL, Credit - Warren Gretz 57

Chapter 4
© Alan and Sandy Carey/Photo Researchers, Inc. 60; PhotoDisc/Getty Images 61; www.istockphoto.com/Sawayasu Tsuji 66 (top); © 2008 JupiterImages Corporation 66 (bottom); © Gerard Fuehrer/Visuals Unlimited 67 (top left); www.istockphoto .com/Oksana Perkins 67 (top right); www .istockphoto.com/Frank Leung 67 (bottom); www.istockphoto.com/Jose Gil 72; © Phil A. Dotson/Photo Researchers, Inc. 73 (left); © Steve and Dave Maslowski/Photo Researchers, Inc. 73 (right); Jeff Henry 74; Getty Images/James Warwick 75; Unusual Films 77

Unit 3 Opener
www.istockphoto.com/Paul LeFevre 81

Chapter 5
Unusual Films 84, 85 (top), 86, 87 (all), 88, 89 (all), 90, 91 (all), 93, 101 (all), 102 (right); Used with permission by Salter Brecknell Weighing Products, a division of Avery Weigh-Tronix, LLC 85 (bottom); sparkia © Fotolia 94; © Mark Sykes/ Alamy 95 (top); Ted Morrison/FoodPix/ JupiterImages Corporation 95 (bottom); © 2008 JupiterImages Corporation 96 (top); www.istockphoto.com/Claudio Arnese 96 (bottom); www.istockphoto.com/Kelly Cline 97; Anne Kitzman © Fotolia 102 (left); Jörg Jahn © Fotolia 103

Chapter 6
Unusual Films 107, 123; Getty Images/ Rubberball/Chris Alvanas 108 (top);

© Stockbyte/Alamy 108 (bottom); Wendyday © Fotolia 109 (top); © TongRo Image Stock/ Alamy 109 (middle); Getty Images/Tom Le Goff 109 (bottom); www.istockphoto.com/ james steidl 110; www.istockphoto.com/ Nick Schlax 112; www.istockphoto.com/ Gordana Sermek 113; © 2008 JupiterImages Corporation 117 (top), 119 (top right, middle, bottom); www.istockphoto.com/Eliza Snow 119 (top left)

Chapter 7
Roman Kadler © Fotolia 128 (left); © Corbis Premium RF/Alamy 128 (right); Biophoto Associates/Photo Researchers, Inc. 129; Unusual Films 131, 135 (top); PhotoDisc, Inc. 134 (top left); choucashoot © Fotolia 134 (bottom left); www.istockphoto.com/Elnur Amikishiyev 134 (bottom right); CORBIS 135 (bottom left); © 2008 JupiterImages Corporation 135 (bottom right), 137 (bottom left); www.istockphoto.com/Kim Bunker 136 (top left); PhotoDisc, Inc. 136 (top right, bottom left, bottom right), 137 (top); Jacek Chabraszewski © Fotolia 137 (bottom middle); www.istockphoto.com/andres balcazar 137 (bottom right); www.istockphoto .com/Wouter van Caspel 138; Marc Dietrich © Fotolia 139 (left); Igor Groshev © Fotolia 139 (middle); zimmytws © Fotolia 139 (right); www.istockphoto.com/clifford shirley 139 (bottom)

Unit 4 Opener
irina2005 © Fotolia 143

Chapter 8
Unusual Films 149, 154 (left), 158 (left, middle), 159 (middle, bottom left), 161; PhotoDisc/Getty Images 150; Stephen Christopher 151; www.istockphoto.com/ Koch Valérie 152; www.istockphoto.com/ Sean Curry 153 (top left); © A. B. Joyce/Photo Researchers, Inc. 153 (top right); © 2008 JupiterImages Corporation 153 (bottom), 157 (middle right); © Albert Copley, OK State/ Images Courtesy AGI Image Bank/http:// www.earthscienceworld.org 154 (right); www.istockphoto.com/Dave Wetzel 155; © USGS/Images Courtesy AGI Image Bank/ http://www.earthscienceworld.org/imagebank/ 157 (top left); Ivik © Fotolia 157 (top right); © Dr. Richard Busch/Images Courtesy AGI

Image Bank/http://www.earthscienceworld.org/ imagebank/ 157 (middle left, bottom left); www.istockphoto.com/Manuela Weschke 157 (bottom right); www.istockphoto.com/Sergey Galushko 158 (right); © Charles D. Winters/ Photo Researchers, Inc. 159 (top); © Raul Gonzalez Perez/Photo Researchers, Inc. 159 (bottom right)

Chapter 9

© 2008 JupiterImages Corporation 165 (top), 166 (top), 178 (top); © ALANDAWSONPHOTOGRAPHY/ Alamy 165 (bottom); dbvirago © Fotolia 166 (bottom); www.istockphoto.com/Marilyn Nieves 167; www.istockphoto.com/Julie Kendall 170 (top); www.istockphoto.com/ Sebastian Santa 170 (bottom); www .istockphoto.com/Erik Kolstad 171 (all); www .istockphoto.com/Duncan Walker 173 (top); www.istockphoto.com/Arturo Limon 173 (bottom); Unusual Films 177; www .istockphoto.com/Clint Spencer 178 (middle); www.istockphoto.com/Brett Charlton 178 (bottom); www.istockphoto.com/Lloyd Paulson 179

Chapter 10

SOHO - EIT Consortium, ESA, NASA [Sun] 183, 185; NASA-GSFC [Earth] 184, 186, 188, 190, 192, 194; USGS/JPL/NASA [Mercury] 184, 186, 188, 190, 192, 194; USGS/JPL/ NASA [Neptune] 184, 187, 189, 191, 193, 194, 195; NASA/JPL/Space Science Institute [Saturn] 184, 187, 189, 191, 193, 195; NASA/ JPL [Jupiter] 185, 187, 189, 190, 191, 193, 195; NASA, ESA, and The Hubble Heritage Team (STScI/AURA) [Mars] 185, 186, 188, 189, 190, 192, 194; © California Association for Research in Astronomy/Photo Researchers, Inc. [Uranus] 185, 187, 189, 191, 193, 194, 195; ArtINeed, Inc. [Venus] 185, 186, 187, 188, 190, 192, 194; NASA/JPL 188 (Moon), 192 (Titan), 193 (Saturn rings), 195 (asteroid), 195 (Pluto); Unusual Films 197; ESO 198

Unit 5 Opener

Rob © Fotolia 201

Chapter 11

Breck P. Kent 204; © MELBA PHOTO AGENCY/Alamy 207 (top), 212 (top); © SPL/Photo Researchers, Inc. 207 (bottom); Unusual Films 211; © Ralph Hutchings/Visuals Unlimited 212 (bottom); Nephron/Wikimedia/GNU Free Documentation License/Creative Commons Attribution-Share Alike 3.0 Unported 213 (bottom)

Chapter 12

© 2008 JupiterImages Corporation 218, 231 (top), 233; Step © Fotolia 220; www. istockphoto.com/Emrah Turudu 222; © ImageState/Media Bakery 223; Unusual Films 225, 231 (bottom); Wikipedia/Ralf Roletschek 227; www.istockphoto.com/Julie Masson Deshaies 232